"This is a closely reasoned and eloquent defense of religious freedom (Guinness calls it 'soul freedom,' because it refers to the rights of secularists as well as people of faith). This is not just one right among many, but a fundamental right rooted in the dignity of every human being. But it is also a right essential to the maintenance of a public space in which people with widely diverse worldviews can live together with civility. This is a book that should be read by everyone concerned with freedom of conscience, not only in the face of murderous persecution as still exists in many places, but also with the more subtle threats by political orthodoxies in Western democracies."

Peter L. Berger, professor emeritus, Boston University, founder and senior research fellow, Institute on Culture, Religion, and World Affairs

"One of the foremost religious-liberty thinkers of our time, Os Guinness sets a soaring goal for this book: establishing a vision of religious freedom ('soul freedom') that accommodates competing truth claims about who man is and why he exists, guarantees freedom and justice, and builds stability amidst a fragile world order. Guinness succeeds magnificently. This book should be required reading for the secularist and the theocrat alike. Its Global Charter of Conscience is a blueprint for all the peoples of the world—both in the West and beyond—struggling to achieve for themselves just and lasting regimes of ordered liberty."

Thomas F. Farr, director, The Religious Freedom Project, Georgetown University's Berkley Center for Religion, Peace, and World Affairs

"For a generation now, Os Guinness has stood as one of our most consistently prophetic voices. In this latest book he returns to a lifelong concern: the precarious status of religious liberty in a fractured world. Drawing on a breadth of insights from history, philosophy, sociology and theology, Guinness makes a compelling case for the primacy of 'soul freedom' as the only enduring foundation for securing peace and human flourishing in our fractious era of unprecedented pluralism. And he does so in his inimitable way, with passion, eloquence and civility. It is a challenging yet ultimately hopeful message that demands to be heard, and to be acted upon."

William Inboden, University of Texas-Austin, former senior director, National Security Council, the White House

"Os Guinness consistently tackles salient and difficult issues and, while giving due recognition to their complexity, analyzes them in clear argument and expounds them in lucid prose. In *The Global Public Square,* he does so again. Contemporary problems of diversity and religious freedom are massive, urgent and growing, but our deep differences are seldom addressed in other than a shallow way. This short but wide-ranging and eloquent defense of freedom of religion and conscience, and civility and plurality—which the author summarizes as 'soul freedom'—provides much-needed insight and guidance in our common future."

Paul Marshall, senior fellow at the Hudson Institute and coauthor of *Silenced: How Apostasy and Blasphemy Codes are Choking Freedom Worldwide*

OS GUINNESS

THE GLOBAL PUBLIC SQUARE

RELIGIOUS FREEDOM AND THE MAKING OF A WORLD SAFE FOR DIVERSITY

IVP Books

An imprint of InterVarsity Press
Downers Grove, Illinois

InterVarsity Press
P.O. Box 1400, Downers Grove, IL 60515-1426
World Wide Web: www.ivpress.com
E-mail: email@ivpress.com

InterVarsity Press® is the book-publishing division of InterVarsity Christian Fellowship/USA®, a
movement of students and faculty active on campus at hundreds of universities, colleges and schools of
nursing in the United States of America, and a member movement of the International Fellowship of
Evangelical Students. For information about local and regional activities, write Public Relations Dept.,
InterVarsity Christian Fellowship/USA, 6400 Schroeder Rd., P.O. Box 7895, Madison, WI 53707-7895,
or visit the IVCF website at <www.intervarsity.org>.

All Scripture quotations, unless otherwise indicated, are taken from the Holy Bible, New International
Version®, NIV® Copyright © 1973, 1978, 1984, 2011 by Biblica, Inc.™ Used by permission. All rights
reserved worldwide.

Every effort has been made to credit all material quoted in this book. Any errors or omissions brought to
the publisher's attention will be corrected in future editions.

Published in association with the literary agency of Wolgemuth & Associates.

Cover design: Cindy Kiple
Interior design: Beth Hagenberg
Images: imagedepotpro/Getty Images

ISBN 978-0-8308-3767-0 (print)
ISBN 978-0-8308-9565-6 (digital)

Printed in the United States of America ∞

Library of Congress Cataloging-in-Publication Data

Guinness, Os.
 The global public square : religious freedom and the making of a world
safe for diversity / Os Guinness.
   pages cm
 Includes bibliographical references.
 ISBN 978-0-8308-3767-0 (pbk. : alk. paper)
 1. Freedom of religion. 2. Liberty of conscience. 3. Liberty. 4.
Human rights. I. Title.
 BL640.G85 2013
 201'.723--dc23
                                                                              2013015235

| P | 19 | 18 | 17 | 16 | 15 | 14 | 13 | 12 | 11 | 10 | 9 | 8 | 7 | 6 | 5 | 4 | 3 | 2 | 1 |
| Y | 29 | 28 | 27 | 26 | 25 | 24 | 23 | 22 | 21 | 20 | 19 | 18 | 17 | 16 | 15 | 14 | 13 |

DOM,
And to CJ, my lionheart of a son,
And his friends, and generation

Thus says the Lord, "Let my people go!"

Moses to the Pharaoh of Egypt, c. 1300 B.C.

It is a fundamental human right that every man should worship according to his own convictions.

Tertullian, *Ad Scapulam*, c. 212

The English Church shall be free, and have its rights undiminished and its liberties unimpaired.

Magna Carta, Runnymede, 1215

The human race is in the best condition when it has the greatest degree of liberty.

Dante Alighieri, *De Monarchia*, 1559

It is the will and command of God that . . . a permission of the most paganish, Jewish, Turkish, or anti-Christian consciences and worships, be granted to all men in all countries: and that they are only to be fought against with that sword which is only (in soul matters) able to conquer, to wit, the sword of God's spirit, the Word of God.

Roger Williams, *The Bloudy Tenent*, 1649

Give me the liberty to know, to utter, and to argue freely according to conscience, above all liberties.

John Milton, *Areopagitica*, 1689

We are right to take alarm at the first experiment upon our liberties.

James Madison, "Memorial and Remonstrance," 1785

To contend for our own liberty, and to deny that blessing to others, involves an inconsistency not to be excused.

John Jay, letter to R. Luhington, 1786

The constitutional freedom of religion [is] the most inalienable and sacred of all human rights.

Thomas Jefferson, Virginia Board of Visitors minutes, 1819

The absolute monarchies have dishonoured despotism. Let us be careful that the democratic republics do not rehabilitate it.

Alexis de Tocqueville, *Democracy in America*, 1840

By birth all men are free.

Lord Acton, *The History of Freedom in Antiquity*, 1877

Freedom means the supremacy of human rights everywhere.

Franklin D. Roosevelt, State of the Union Address, 1941

These are the rights of all human beings. They are yours whoever you are. Demand that your rulers and politicians sign and observe this declaration. If they refuse, if they quibble, they can have no place in the new free world that dawns upon mankind.

H. G. Wells, *Rights of the World Citizen*, 1942

Everyone has the right to freedom of thought, conscience and religion; this right includes freedom to change his religion or belief, and freedom, either in community with others and in public or private, to manifest his religion or belief in teaching, practice, worship, and observance.

Universal Declaration of Human Rights, Article 18, 1948

The General Assembly proclaims this Universal Declaration of Human Rights as a common standard of achievement for all peoples and all nations, to the end that every individual and every organ of society, keeping this Declaration constantly in mind, shall strive by teaching and education to promote respect for these rights and freedoms and by progressive measures, national and international, to secure their universal and effective recognition and observance, both among peoples of the member states themselves and among the peoples under their jurisdiction.

Universal Declaration of Human Rights, 1948

So, let us not be blind to our differences—but let us also direct our attention to our common interests and to means by which those differences can be resolved. And if we cannot end now our differences, at least we can help make the world safe for diversity. For, in the final analysis, our most basic common link is that we all inhabit this planet. We all breathe the same air. We all cherish our children's future. And we are all mortal.

President John F. Kennedy, Commencement Address at American University, 1963

The Universal Declaration of Human Rights states a common understanding of the peoples of the world concerning the inalienable and inviolable rights of all members of the human family and constitutes an obligation for the members of the international community.

Tehran International Conference on Human Rights, 1968

Freedom of thought, conscience and religion is one of the foundations of a democratic society.

European Court of Human Rights, 1993

Relativism is incapable of defending anything, including itself. When a society loses its soul, it is about to lose its future.

Rabbi Jonathan Sacks, 2011

Religious freedom is a moral and political good for all human beings and all societies.

Thomas Farr, Georgetown University, 2012

Contents

1

THE GOLDEN KEY

Soul Freedom for All

WE ARE NOW SEVEN BILLION humans jostling together on our tiny planet earth, up from a mere two and a half billion in the lifetime of many living today. Small and insignificant perhaps in contrast to the vastness of the cosmos, we face a simple but profound challenge: *How do we live with our deepest differences, especially when those differences are religious and ideological, and very especially when those differences concern matters of our common public life? In short, how do we create a global public square and make the world safer for diversity?*

The answer to this titanic challenge requires an answer to the prior question of who we humans think we are, and then attending closely to the dictates of our humanity. Put differently, we face a triple imperative that will be a key to our human future: First, to see whether we have reason enough to believe in the measureless dignity and worth of every last one of us. Second, to know whether we can discover a way to live with the deepest differences that divide us. Third, to find out whether we are able to settle our deliberations and debates in public life through reasoned persuasion rather than force, intimidation and violence—even in the age of the new media and a global resurgence of religion.

Indispensable to solving these challenges is the extension of *soul freedom* for all. Soul freedom is the inviolable freedom of thought, conscience, religion and belief that alone does full justice to the dictates of our humanity. As we shall see, it best expresses human dignity and agency; it promotes freedom and justice for all; it fosters healthy giving, caring, peaceful and stable societies; and it acts as a bulwark against the countless current abuses of power and the equally countless brutal oppressions of human dignity.

As such, soul freedom concerns the foundational freedom to be human. It is both the expression of a high view of human worth and the answer to a human yearning for freedom that is universal and enduring, as well as the surest bulwark against the darker angels of our nature. Soul freedom rises to the challenge of the dictates of our humanity because it is about nothing less than our freedom and responsibility to be fully human and to live together in thriving and beneficial communities, and at the same time to know how to lean against the crooked timber that is also at the heart of our humanity.

Soul freedom for all was once attacked as naive and utopian, and it is still resisted as subversive. Yet it is not only a shining ideal but a dire necessity today and an eminently practical solution to the predicaments of our time. Truly it is the golden key to a troublesome situation in which the darker angels must not be allowed to dominate.

For as the present world situation shows only too clearly, the emerging global era is a time of deep anxieties and fears for governments, groups and individuals. Out of this state of mind many follies and some great dangers and disasters are growing, and we are not far removed from the false and barbarously inhuman answers of the twentieth century. The natural personal desire for certainty and the natural government and group desire for unity can each in their way be twisted into overreaching demands for uniformity, and then into a remorseless slide toward coercive conformity that too often ends with raw power as the abuser of human freedom, justice, security and well-being. Add to this the clash of religions and ideologies, the cacophony of the new media, and the high-octane dimension of prejudice and hatred, and the combination can be lethal.

Against all such abuses, whether by governments, religions, ideologies, tyrants, bureaucrats, university administrators, towering individual egos or some politically correct orthodoxy of one kind or another, this work is a passionate cry for soul freedom for all—for every single person on the earth—and a call to see how its freedom of thought, conscience, religion and belief may be advanced in the world of today and tomorrow for the sake of the true dictates of our humanity.

Soul freedom for all stands as the supreme challenge to all contemporary forms of dictatorship of the mind and heart, whether secularist totalitarianism of the Chinese and North Korean kind, or religious authoritarianism of the Iranian, Saudi and Burmese kind. As such, soul freedom is as realistic as it is idealistic. It speaks to the best and guards against the worst of human nature. It not only stands against open dictatorships but mounts a clear warning to all the rising forms of Western illiberalism, especially those that spring from the zealotry of good intentions.

In the short term, soul freedom is essential if there is to be a positive answer to three of the greatest questions shaping the future in the coming century: Will Islam modernize peacefully? Which faith will replace Marxism in China? And will the West sever or recover its roots?

In the long term, soul freedom is crucial to whether there will be an expansion or a rollback of human rights and responsibilities across the earth, and therefore to the prospects for freedom, justice, conscience, human dignity and human well-being itself.

In particular, soul freedom for all must now be freshly understood and advanced in the Western world if it is to hold its indispensable place throughout the whole world. For if the present erosions continue, Western claims about freedom, democracy and progress will slowly be rendered hollow, and the West will be the west in geography only. After all, soul freedom has long been left half-baked and poorly protected in countries such as England, where it was once pioneered, and there are major problems with its status in many countries across Europe.

Yet that is nothing compared with the specter that now looms across the Atlantic. For if soul freedom continues to be neglected and threatened in the United States as it has been recently, it clearly can be endangered anywhere. Fine words are not enough. The wordsmiths of the world have been busy, but statesmen have been absent, lawyers have run amok and activists have trampled the ground carelessly in their rush to press their own interests. Only wise leadership and courageous action can bring the situation back and lead us forward. The stakes for the world and the future of humanity are incalculable.

The immensity of the issue has been created by the clash of three trends that every concerned citizen of the world must recognize and confront:

- First, there is now solid and incontrovertible evidence that when freedom of thought, conscience, religion and belief is recognized, respected and advanced for citizens of all faiths and none, there is a parallel advance in many important social goods, such as peace, stability, social cohesion, generosity, enterprise and the unleashing of the positive forces of civil society.[1]

- Second, there is equally strong but contrary evidence that restrictions on this foundational human right are a mounting problem across most of the nations of the world, including countries that were once the leading champions of this freedom.[2] The plain fact is that the overwhelming majority of the world's people believe strongly in *someone or something higher than human*, yet the overwhelming majority of them do not have the freedom to practice their faith freely. In 2010, for the very first time, the United States moved into the top sixteen countries of the world where there was a rise in both government restrictions and social hostility toward religion.[3]

- Third, the greatest current obstacle to resolving these contradictory trends is a surprising one. The menace to religious freedom is no longer just the age-old evils of authoritarian oppression and sectarian violence around the world, but a grave new menace from within the West itself. For we are seeing an unwitting convergence between some very different Western trends that together form a perfect storm. One trend is the general disdain for religion that leads to a discounting of religious freedom, sharpened by a newly aggressive atheism and a heavy-handed separationism that both call for the exclusion of religion from public life. Another is the overzealous attempt of certain activists of the sexual revolution to treat freedom of religion and belief as an obstruction to their own rights that must be dismantled forever. Yet another is the sometimes blatant, sometimes subtle initiatives of certain advocates of Islam to press their own claims in ways that contradict freedom of religion and belief, and freedom of speech as it has been classically understood. (Current Western forms of hate speech, for example, operate in a similar way to the blasphemy laws put forward on behalf of Islam, and they are equally misguided.) Each of these trends represents a serious crisis in itself. But when considered together, and especially in light of the generally maladroit governmental responses, they are also a window into the decline of the West.

In 2015, the world will celebrate the eight hundredth anniversary of Magna Carta, the iconic charter of English liberties imposed upon King John at Runnymede in 1215. Winston Churchill described it as "the charter of every self-respecting man at any time in any land."[4] But if the celebration is not to be hollow, we must use the occasion to assess the current dangers and obstacles to freedom, take stock of our liberties and rights, and see where we have slipped and where we need to advance, even in the lands that once pioneered these precious and essential human freedoms.

THE CRUNCH GENERATION

"If you could be born in any generation other than your own, which would you choose?" I was first asked that question at Stanford University, and I hesitated before replying. What did the questioner have in mind? My family is Irish, but I was born in China and spent my first ten years there, and since then I have lived in Europe and North America and visited many other parts of the world in both hemispheres. Possible responses flashed through my mind, ranging from the Athens of Pericles to the Rome of the Emperor Hadrian, to the China of the Tang or Ming dynasties, to the Florence of Lorenzo de' Medici, to the America of George Washington, Thomas Jefferson, John Adams and James Madison, and the England of William Pitt and William Wilberforce. But almost instantly I knew my answer before I had time to debate these other periods.

"Your generation," I said. "I would like to be a member of your generation because in your lifetime you will witness some of the most crucial years humanity has ever navigated."

The present generation now rising to its early adulthood across the earth can be described as "the crunch generation" because of the present state of the global era and the many crucial issues converging to challenge humankind. In his last speech to the British House of Commons, Winston Churchill asked the question "What if God tires of the human race?" He was referring to the apocalyptic possibilities of the nuclear issue in the 1960s. Today, a generation later, a wide raft of issues—economic, technological, demographic, social, political, medical, environmental, as well as nuclear—is crowding in to menace the horizons of the world that is almost at the door.

If the coming generation answers these issues responsibly and well, the world can look forward to calmer sailing. But if they are answered badly or not at all, the prospects for the future and for the future of humankind are turbulent.

What then do we face? An inspiring new era for global humanity, a new dark age for the earth or a period of muddling through that lies somewhere in between? Only God knows the answer. Futurism is a murky science that often pretends to know far more than it does, but there are certain issues and certain problems that are clear beyond dispute. This book is about one of the biggest of them, the challenge facing all of us as the earth's now billions of citizens: *Soul freedom for all and its answer to how we are to maximize freedom and justice and learn to live with our deepest differences, especially when those differences are religious and ideological—and in particular the answer to how we are to negotiate those differences in public life, and so create a global public square that is worthy of our heritage as members of free and open societies.*

Immediate reactions to that statement may vary, but it is hardly a secret that many of the world's educated people respond with weariness, if not disgust, at any mention of religion. Anything to do with religion and public affairs is messy at best and repugnant at worst. But while the issue is awkward and difficult, there is no avoiding it. Incidents of egregious violations of freedom of thought, conscience, religion and belief are coming in from all around the world, and urgent analyses and reports are mounting too.[5] It is now said that more than one billion people live under governments that systematically suppress freedom of religion and belief, and that 70 percent of the world's seven billion people are living in countries with a high degree of restrictions on their faith, which in turn means injustice and suffering for millions and millions.

Responsible leaders, as well citizens, can no longer ignore this issue, for it represents not only a massive denial of individual freedom but a major humanitarian crisis and a grand strategic challenge to global peace and security.[6] But what follows is not merely one more analysis or one more protest, important though these may be. Progress surely requires that the first step toward answering any serious problem is to go beyond the point at which we started. What is offered here is an exploration of an indispensable key to the future, and one that sets out a proposal for a constructive way forward for humankind, with three different components:

- *First, a vision of soul freedom for all, the foundational freedom of thought, conscience, religion and belief that reflects, promotes and protects the inviolable and alienable dignity and worth of all human beings.*

- *Second, a proposal for cultivating civility and constructing a global public square that maximizes soul freedom for people of all faiths and none, and shows how such a vision can do justice to the integrity of diverse truth claims while also guaranteeing freedom and building stability.*

- *Third, to support these two goals, a Global Charter of Conscience that reaffirms Article 18 of the Universal Declaration of Human Rights and sets out its significance for establishing and protecting soul freedom in the world of today.*

FOR WHOM AND BY WHOM?

We live in a cynical age well schooled in suspicion and well stocked with reasons to be suspicious. Our first instincts are therefore to look for the bottom line and the real agenda. And that in fact is not all bad, for soul freedom is not a utopian daydream but a vision of freedom carved out against the realism of what Immanuel Kant called the "crooked timber" of our humanity. Let me then put my cards on the table at the outset.

Who is this book written for? On the one hand, this book attempts to set out a vision of liberty and justice throughout the earth and for all human beings. No single person can ever speak on behalf of all humanity, for the obvious reason that none of us can speak from everywhere any more than we can speak from nowhere. We all speak from somewhere, but it is possible to speak for what are sincerely believed to be the best interests of all, and thus for the common good, the good of everyone. In that sense, although I cannot do other than write as a single individual and from the perspective of my own faith and my own place in the world, this book is written for Asians as much as Europeans, for Middle Easterners, Africans and Latin Americans as much as North Americans. It is written for atheists and Muslims, for Hindus and Buddhists, for Mormons and Baha'i, and for the adherents of every faith under the sun, as much as for Jews and Christians.

Importantly, this book is written for individual believers as well as for the religious and ideological institutions and the organizations behind them. And most importantly too, it is written for liberals and conservatives alike, though it challenges equally the unconservative actions of some conservatives and the illiberal actions of some liberals.

On the other hand, and with a closer focus, this book is addressed especially to those people across the world who are concerned for global as well as national affairs and feel the force of three basic things:

- First, the inescapable fact of the world's diversity, part promise and part problem
- Second, the prime values of freedom, justice and order to humanity in any age
- Third, the menace of the many-sided threats to human thought and conscience today

This proposal shares with many people the stubborn hope that drift and disaster need not be the last word in the human story. Here, for all who appreciate such core realities, is a vision, an argument and a practical proposal that set out a possible way forward for humanity on a crucial issue and at a critical juncture of world history.

And who is this book written by? I write as a Christian, a follower of Jesus of Nazareth. Had all who bore the name Christian been true to the teaching and the way of Jesus himself, that identification might cause no problem and raise no suspicion. But tragically a significant part of the religious repressions and bloodshed throughout history have been perpetrated by those who called themselves Christian and did what they did in the name of Jesus. From the dark record of the Inquisition and the slaughter of the Albigensians and the Huguenots, to the infamous papal attacks on religious freedom in the nineteenth century and down to the far slighter follies and fears raised by the so-called Christian right in recent American history, Christians have too often been or been seen as part of the problem and not the solution. As a Woody Allen character says in his film *Hannah and Her Sisters*, "If Jesus were to come back and see what people have done in his name, he'd throw up."

Indeed, it is only fair to acknowledge frankly that a significant reason for the present aggressiveness of many secularists toward religion is their legitimate reaction to the past corruptions and oppressions of the state churches in Europe, and to the fear that such things might happen again. The Enlightenment philosopher Denis Diderot seconded Jean Meslier's conviction that the world would be happy only when "the last king has been strangled with the guts of the last priest." Gruesome as it sounds, and bloody though the fulfillment turned out to be for the Bourbons and the aristocratic class, that desire represented a passionate cry for freedom and justice and an accurate indictment of the brutal repressions of both throne and altar under the ancien régime in France.[7]

The time has come for atheists to define themselves by what they believe rather than what they disbelieve. After several centuries they have made the point clearly that they are not theists, and most of the rest of us are happy to accept their assertion. But at the same time they are not really "nones" either, and their faith, which is far from vacuous, needs spelling out. But a plausible case can be made, and I for one am equally happy to grant it, that whatever their vision of life without God, gods or the supernatural, most forms of secularism are also fueled in large part by an understandable reaction to the excesses and evils of religion. Much of the world can agree on this with no further argument: bad religion is very bad indeed.

Yet the teaching of Jesus himself points in an entirely different direction than much of Christendom. Not only has Pope John Paul II, as leader of the worst offender among the Christian traditions, openly confessed the past sins of the Roman Catholic Church, but there are powerful branches of the Christian community who have always tried to follow Jesus more directly, who have never had blood on their hands, and who have a shining record in standing for human rights in general and for the cause of freedom of conscience in particular.

Indeed, the name and the notion of soul freedom come from Roger Williams's iconic term *soul liberty*. He was the seventeenth-century English dissenter who was an inspiring pioneer of both freedom and freedom of thought, conscience and religion for all, and his courageous stand deserves far wider recognition and celebration. He, and not Thomas Jefferson, was the first person to call for "a wall of separation" between church and state, to devise the world's first government that enshrined that principle, and to offer freedom of thought, conscience and religion to people of all faiths and none—without exception.[8]

Besides, the Christian faith is the first truly global religion, the leading proponent of the three great Abrahamic faiths, by far the world's most numerous and diverse, and also at the moment by far the most persecuted. As I write, the U.S. Commission on International Human Rights has issued its report listing sixteen countries as the worst violators of religious freedom, and while many religions are persecuted in these countries and elsewhere, only Christians are persecuted in all of them.[9] All that to say that there can be no solution to the world's problem without significant Christian participation.

Speaking for myself, I emphatically challenge the disdain that views all religion as uncouth and unworthy of serious understanding. I equally reject the current sneer that to defend freedom of religion and belief is merely a covert form of advancing faith of one kind or another. From the drafting of the Williamsburg Charter, which celebrated and reaffirmed the First Amendment to the U.S. Constitution, to the drafting of the Global Charter of Conscience, which was published in Brussels in 2012 to reaffirm Article 18 of the Universal Declaration of Human Rights, I have long joined forces to work with all who defend the human rights of all human beings—all human rights and all human beings without exception, but with a special eye to the foundational importance of freedom of thought, conscience, religion and belief.

So let the past and the suspicions that it stirs be put to one side for the moment, and let this present proposal speak for itself and be judged on its own merits. For a start, there needs to be a clear understanding of what soul freedom is and is not, and this needs to be augmented by a realistic dealing with the many obstacles seen to be standing in its way. Together this clarity and this realism can open the way to an innovative and constructive approach to what is a vital requirement for our human future.

What Kind of a World Community?

At point after point after point, a simple but profound question rises out of the issues confronting the world in the global era: What kind of a world community do we want to build and live in together? There can be no good answer to this question unless we first resolve the issue of living with our deep differences, and currently there are few solutions on offer.

What follows is one proposal for a constructive solution and an exploration of eight steps that are needed if we are to rethink the issue. If taken together, these steps could achieve a grand global revaluation that would usher in the possibility of a robustly healthy multifaith world that comes nearer than any so far to advancing freedom and justice under the conditions of advanced modern pluralism. The time has come to face down the ugly crowd of prejudices that clamor around this issue, and then to rescue the freedom and the right of soul freedom and place them at the heart of the global discussion where they belong. How we deal with our deepest religious and ideological differences in public life will be a defining issue for the future of humankind.

It is time, and past time, to ponder the question. What does it say of us and our times that the Universal Declaration of Human Rights could not be passed today? And what does it say of the future of freedom of thought, conscience, religion and belief if it can be neglected and threatened even in the United States, where it once developed most fully—that it can be endangered anywhere? Who will step forward now to champion the cause of freedom for the good of all and for the future of humanity?

2

FOR ALL
THE WORLD

THE FIRST STEP IN THE REVALUATION *is to recognize that
soul freedom is for the good of all, down to the very last human
person, that educated elites in the Western world must overcome their
personal prejudices about religion in order to take it as seriously as it
deserves, and that no solution will be possible without a partnership
between responsible religious believers and responsible secularists.*

The term *religious freedom* was first used by Tertullian, a
Christian apologist in the third century. But it has been argued that
the long, hard quest for freedom of thought, conscience, religion
and belief goes back all the way to the Jewish conception of humanity made in the image of God—and in particular to their historic exodus from Egypt under the ringing cry of Moses to the
Pharaoh, "Let my people go!" Judaism is the religion of freedom
and responsibility par excellence. No people have suffered more
than the Jews, yet no people have done more for the freedom of the
world, not only through their history but through the beliefs and
ideas they have brought into the world and sustained down the
centuries. But wherever the rise of freedom may be traced, it is

certainly true that the rise and recognition of the freedom and the right has never progressed in an unbroken straight line, and it did not come from a simple discovery of truths that were courageously won and then never lost.

The long, painful struggle for freedom included lurches and setbacks along the way, and the victories owed much to a tug of war between passionate ideas on one side and powerful interests on the other. Thus human rights are a part of the ceaseless, ongoing struggle between *right* and *might*, *conscience* and *reason*, *principle* and *policy*. A celebrated example of mixed motives was France's Edict of Toleration in 1598 after Henry IV had earlier switched faiths from Huguenot to Catholic. "Paris is well worth a mass," he is supposed to have said. In the end, Henry the royal Catholic convert was assassinated by a fellow Catholic, and his edict was later revoked by a royal successor, but the edict was still a significant landmark in the slow emergence of toleration for all believers.

In particular, the rise and recognition of freedom of conscience represents a complex interaction between three factors:

- The growing assertion of human rights, such as freedom of conscience, freedom of expression and freedom of association

- The equally important adjustment to social realities, such as the expanding pluralism in modern countries

- The far more variable facts of political regulations, according to the personal interests of kings, cardinals, governors, judges and university deans—or modern politicians eyeing interest groups and electoral votes

For their own pragmatic reasons, leaders of nations down the ages could decide either to relax regulations and allow more freedom, or to tighten them up and enforce more rigid conformity. Interestingly, those who increased toleration, such as Henry IV of France and William of Orange in the Netherlands, usually had multiple motives, whereas those who sought to coerce conformity often did so out of a single-minded obsession. In fact, a common feature of those who deny freedom of conscience in their pursuit of conformity is intransigence, personal or bureaucratic. This is true not only of Louis XIV's draconian revocation of the Edict of Nantes in 1685, but also of the heavy-handed denials of freedom of conscience by equality commissioners and university administrations today.

Against all such intransigence and its repressions of freedom, this book unashamedly argues for right over might and principle over policy. It affirms the primacy of *soul freedom for all, and for the good of all,* and therefore for people of all faiths and none. No one should miss the importance of those last four words. On the one hand, soul freedom reaches out to all religious believers. Freedom of thought, conscience, religion and belief is for all religious believers and is opposed to none. On the other hand, and let there be no misunderstanding here, it reaches out to secularists too, and to any who do not believe in God, gods or the supernatural. *Soul freedom includes all ultimate beliefs and worldviews, whether religious or nonreligious, transcendent or naturalistic.*

Allow me, then, to set out the principles and pitfalls of soul freedom, and the prospects for a global public square that does justice to what Britain's chief rabbi, Lord Sacks, admirably calls "the dignity of difference," and therefore achieves a growing measure of cosmopolitan civility—and show how it realistically can be built over the course of the next generation.[1]

At the same time, this argument recognizes the strong social, political and technological tides now running against freedom, and it is important to identify the powerful undertow of these factors, regardless of whether their source is comfortably distant or awkwardly close to home. Readers of this book will be among the world's educated—if only because it requires literacy and education to read a book of serious ideas. Today, however, that by itself raises an immediate barrier against this argument. For we are at a curious and unusual place in history where many of the world's most literate and tolerant people can become the world's most illiterate and intolerant when it comes to the subject of this book—religion and religious differences.

As we shall see repeatedly, a prominent feature of the problem in the Western world is that where there is a disdain for religion, there is often a discounting of religious freedom too. The first may be understandable, but the second is inexcusable. If the overwhelming majority of the world's peoples firmly believe in someone or something higher than themselves, and yet almost the same overwhelming majority also faces mounting restrictions on their ability to practice the faith in which they believe, there is something wrong with this situation, and that something must be changed. It is unquestionable that freedom of religion and belief includes secularists, but by the same token freedom of religion and belief must be taken seriously by secularists too.

RELIGION—TOGETHER WE CAN FIND THE CURE

Does it betray a deficiency of humanity to fail to acknowledge features of humanity that are common to most human beings? That is too harsh, but it is worth stating simply why the issue of religious differences is important, even for people who, as an article of their own faith, summarily dismiss all religion as unworthy of serious consideration. Call religion stupid, call it reactionary, call it evil or call it any of the names by which it is dismissed today in intellectual circles, but there are reasons why it would be madness beyond folly to ignore the place and role of religion in human affairs.

Unfortunately, atheism today is as badly served by certain strident and intolerant atheists as religion is by certain of its worst proponents. Psychiatrist Iain McGilchrist states what is obvious to

all but those referred to: "In the field of religion there are dogma-
tists of no-faith as there are of faith."[2] Rabbi and philosopher Jonathan Sacks puts the point with equal bluntness:

> Atheism deserves better than the new atheists whose method-
> ology consists in criticizing religion without understanding it,
> quoting texts without contexts, taking exceptions as the rule,
> confusing folk belief with reflective theology, abusing, mocking,
> ridiculing, caricaturing and demonizing religious faith and
> holding it responsible for all the crimes against humanity.[3]

But with the new atheists dominating intellectual opinion in
much of the Western world and calling crudely for the end of faith,
it bears repeating why freedom of thought, conscience, religion
and belief is vital for the good of all—even for those who disagree
with religion.

First, soul freedom, as the answer to how we live with our
deepest differences, is vital because negotiating diversity underlies
so many of the other great issues in the global era. It may sound
abstract and far less important than other urgent problems such as
terrorism, famine, HIV/AIDS, nuclear proliferation, environmental
degradation and shortages of water. But how we live with our
deepest differences lies behind so many of the other issues and the
way they will be handled. It is therefore crucial and indispensable
for answering the others—a golden key to the future, though to a
troublesome problem.

Without freedom of thought, conscience, religion and belief, the
escalating culture warring that we already see in many advanced
modern countries could spread. We may see a plague of global tensions that could wrack the world and block any progress toward a
wiser future for humankind.

Second, soul freedom, as the answer to how we live with our
deepest differences, is vital because it touches on the quest for cer-

tainty by countless numbers of humans today. For the vast majority of humanity throughout history as well as today, religion has been and still is the ultimate belief that is the very deepest source of human meaning and belonging. Soul freedom, or freedom of thought and conscience, which includes religion and ideology, is therefore foundational and precious to all human beings. It touches on the deepest roots of the meaning and belonging that makes life livable in ways that science alone can never satisfy or even address.

That simple anthropological fact about religion, meaning and belonging has been reinforced today by history, sociology and the cognitive sciences. It is reason enough to take religion seriously, even when disagreeing with it. Nothing is more essential and precious to humans than meaning and belonging, nothing is easier and more natural than answering the ultimate questions through religion, nothing is more vital than freedom of thought and conscience in dealing with meaning and belonging, and nothing is more dangerous than to twist or suppress the human desire for certainty over meaning and belonging. All this should at least be remembered and respected by those who disagree with religion vehemently, and especially by any who have strong aversion to particular religions.

To dismiss all religion without a thought, as if all religions were the same, and as if the critics' own philosophies of life were not the functional equivalent of religion, is a thoughtlessness bordering on contempt for our human need for meaning and belonging. Religious believers often need reminding that freedom of thought, conscience, religion and belief includes the nonreligious and the antireligious, but the nonreligious and the antireligious also need reminding that their secularist beliefs are ultimate beliefs too.

In today's world it is unself-critical as well as elitist and parochial to dismiss religious beliefs out of hand. No one who understands the state of modern philosophy, for example, can ignore the powerful and sophisticated arguments of eminent modern philosophers such as Alasdair MacIntyre, Alvin Plantinga, Richard Swinburne and Nicholas Wolterstorff, all of whom provide powerful rational justification for a warranted faith. It is also foolish to discount faith at the practical level. There is no solid reason to think that humanity will change over this issue. Current talk of a "religionless world" and the "end of faith" is little more than propaganda and wishful thinking, and the claim that religion in the modern world is simply "vestigial" and a "remnant state" left over from earlier times will prove no better.[4] With due respect to the diehard advocates of the secularization thesis, religion shows no sign of disappearing from the earth and is not likely to.

Without freedom of thought and conscience, all distortions or denials of the human need for certainty spawn a breeding ground for restlessness, fanaticism and conflict.

Third, soul freedom, as the answer to how we live with our deepest differences, is vital because it touches on many nonreligious and pragmatic considerations that are crucial for governments and the ordering of nations. As the history of religious freedom proves beyond a doubt, vital secular interests are at stake in settling this issue—such as peace, social harmony, stability, political liberties, favorable business conditions, economic prosperity, success in handling immigration, democratic development and longevity, and even lower infant mortality. Correlation between freedom of thought, conscience and religion and these social goods does not mean causality, but what links many of these issues and makes a successful outcome important is the fact that they depend on how diversity is managed. Coerce conformity and stifle diversity and there will be damaging consequences, even in nonreligious spheres such as the economy.

The lesson of history is clear on this point, amplified most loudly in the blunders of James I and Charles I of England over the Puritans who left to flourish in America, and the equal blunders of Louis XIV and Cardinal Mazarin of France who drove out the Huguenots and helped to sap their own strength and boost the fortunes of their national rivals, the Dutch and the English. It should be pondered by all who would drive religion from public life and from society today.

Without freedom of thought, conscience and religion, all drives toward conformity—whether from totalitarian governments, liberal universities or the gatekeepers of our public squares—end in some degree of coercion that stifles not only freedom but many secular considerations that are more crucial to the powers-that-be than religion itself.

That lesson is as vital today as in the seventeenth century, and it needs to be learned again, not only by Chinese dictators, Saudi kings and Iranian ayatollahs, but by European and American equality commissioners and university administrators. When the religious insistence on monopoly, the communist demand for uniformity and the laudable liberal desire for equality slide into a remorseless drive for conformity, the coercive conformity that results will always prove stifling and self-defeating.

Soul freedom can never be denied without a steep price for individuals, for universities, for entire countries and for humanity. Yet champions of human rights face a major challenge today, for freedom of thought, conscience, religion and belief has plummeted in elite estimation along with the educated world's attitude to religion itself—and as we shall see, all human rights are the losers. Once again, where religion is disdained, freedom of religion and belief is discounted.

WE ARE ALL MADE WITH CROOKED TIMBER

This general point about taking religion seriously needs underscoring gently but firmly or the argument stops here. For better or worse the world is simply not likely to become religionless, yet that is the unexamined faith of many of the world's educated people. "This would be the best of all possible worlds if there were no religion in it," wrote John Adams.[5] His famous comment, taken from his exchange of letters with Thomas Jefferson, is often quoted with relish by critics of religion. Here surely is a distinguished Enlightenment precursor to John Lennon's "Imagine," with its dream of a world with "no religion too." Here, for the sophisticated, is an American founder's unguarded admission of the true menace of religion and a sly endorsement of a religionless world beyond the superstitions of the eighteenth century and the fanaticisms of the twenty-first. A *bon mot* from a philosophe with a Boston accent, an antidote to the cloying civic pieties of other American founders such as George Washington and Alexander Hamilton—what more could an ardent atheist want in the unending battle against the ignorance of the uncouth and the troublesome global resurgence of religions?

After all, for the last quarter of a century it would have been a safe but sad bet that at any moment someone somewhere in the world was killing someone else in the name of religion. Think of the blood-stained arc of violence set off between religions and within religions: Sunni against Shia in Iraq; Muslims against Baha'i in Iran, Copts in Egypt, and Christians in Nigeria; Hindus against Christians in India and Buddhists in Sri Lanka; Orthodox against Muslims in the Balkans; and Protestants and Roman Catholics against each other in Ulster.

Think too of the religiously motivated assassinations of India's prime minister Indira Gandhi, Egypt's president Anwar Sadat, and Israel's prime minister Yitzhak Rabin. Or remember the murder of courageous leaders such as Salmaan Taseer, the Punjab governor slain by his own bodyguards in 2011 for opposing blasphemy laws, and Shahbaz Bhatti, Pakistan's minister of minorities, who was the

Martin Luther King of Pakistan, and like King paid with his life for
standing for the right of freedom of thought and conscience for all.

The religious rage is one thing, and the social and legal responses
are another. When Salmaan Taseer's killer was arrested and sentenced, the courtroom was attacked and ransacked and the judge
fled into hiding out of fear for his life. So much for the rule of law
in the face of religious rage.

And so it goes.

In fact, horrific as it is, such sectarian violence is only the beginning of the problem, and we need to be clear about all of them
from the start. There are three major sources of the menace to
freedom of thought and conscience today:

- Government suppression of religion and ideology—such as the
  harsh Chinese repression of Christians, Muslims, Tibetan Buddhists and the Falun Gong over the last fifty years, the systematic Burmese suppression of the Rohingya Muslims, the
  brutal Iranian persecution of Christians and Baha'i since Ayatollah Khomeini's triumph in Iran in 1979, and the dire restrictions on the Ahmadiyya in Pakistan and Indonesia

- Ethnic and sectarian violence—such as the previous examples
  or the Hindu nationalist massacre of Christians and Muslims
  and the Boko Haram's war against Christians by Muslims in Nigeria, where more than fifty thousand people have been killed
  since 1999

- The worsening conflicts over freedom of thought, conscience,
  religion and belief in the widening series of discriminatory violations in the Western culture wars

The menace from the third source may appear trivial and far less
threatening than the other two. To be sure, such Western violations of thought and freedom of conscience are small compared
with the brutal government repression and bloody sectarian vio-

lence elsewhere in the world. They also have a greater number of different reasons behind them (and therefore potential excuses), ranging from sheer ignorance about freedom of conscience to ideological prejudices, to a crisis of confidence in the Western identity, to a craven desire to appease certain global interests such as oil.

But in truth the mounting Western violations are just as dangerous to soul freedom as the other two sources, both now and in the future. Years of culture warring in the West have now been waged for half a century in the United States itself, with the heat turned up in election years. They have caused an escalating crossfire between the two sides, and the previously shared respect for religious freedom has been left a casualty in the middle. As we shall see in a later chapter, we have reached the dangerous point where certain Western liberals are busily undermining freedom of religion and belief, and certain Western conservatives are equally busy defending it in a way that does it no credit. The result is a tragedy for human rights in general, and for freedom of thought, conscience, religion and belief in particular.

- First, many elites in the Western culture wars display the same disregard for freedom of religion and belief that lies behind the more egregious outrages in authoritarian and totalitarian countries. In France, for example, government restrictions have increased to the point that they exceed Cuba in that category.

- Second, the present disregard for freedom of religion and belief represents hypocrisy and an abject failure of countries that pride themselves on being open, free and champions of human rights, yet are not living up to their claims and their heritage. In Britain, for example, social hostility toward religion has risen so sharply that the British stand with Iran in the category of high social hostility toward religion.

- Third, the sorry result of this disregard is that the Western world is failing to demonstrate a solid alternative to the conflict, violence and oppression elsewhere, and is therefore failing in its responsibility to point the way forward for humankind.

At our present moment in global affairs, these signal failures in the West may look small in comparison with the repressions, persecutions, massacres, rape, torture and executions elsewhere. But unless they are reversed, they will prove to be of titanic significance in the future. James Madison's warning in his "Memorial and Remonstrance" in 1785 cannot be repeated too often: "We are right to take alarm at the first experiment upon our liberties."

Everyone concerned for human dignity and human rights should know beyond a shadow of doubt that we are at a crucial moment for freedom of religion and belief in the history of humankind. It is said that every single current nation in the world now has language about freedom of religion and belief in its constitution, and 143 of the 198 nations also have such language in their basic laws. Yet more than half of these same nations have other statements in their constitutions and laws that contradict freedom of religion and belief. It is therefore clear that persecution and repression are rife throughout the world, and that one third of the world's nations and nearly two thirds of the world's people live in countries with "high restrictions on religion."[6]

Behind the bare facts of this worldwide suppression of freedom of religion and belief are countless untold experiences of grave injustice and deep human suffering. For those with eyes to see and hearts to care, the blood and tears of millions still cry out.

Plainly this is no time to sleep or to avert our eyes. All of us require not only vigilance but a modicum of honesty over this issue. A moment's thought would show that while religion must be held accountable for the worst of the ugly record of sectarian violence, as in Iran, Pakistan and Nigeria, antireligious sources must be held accountable for much of the government repression, as in China and North Korea. And when it comes to the Western culture wars, the fault for the shamefully unnecessary violations of soul freedom must be laid at the doors of liberals and secularists just as much as religious believers.

This is not an argument for moral equivalence, and there is no getting around the fact that religiously motivated sectarian violence is a witches' brew of ancient hatreds and a humanitarian nightmare for humanity. Look at that source alone, and who need look further for proof positive of Christopher Hitchens's bitter accusation that "religion poisons everything"?[7] At the very least, it is all the evidence you need for Blaise Pascal's observation that "Men never delight in doing evil as much as when they can do it for religious reasons."[8] Do evil in the name of God and you can square a moral circle. The evil can be wicked and worthy at the same time. "When religion goes wrong," Archbishop William Temple lamented, "it goes very wrong." The prospect of Adams's religionless world is perhaps worth considering.

Yet not so fast. Former U.S. Secretary of State Madeleine Albright reminds us in her memoir, *The Mighty and the Almighty*, that to use John Adams to argue for a religionless world is a gross distortion of what the second president of the United States actually wrote. The full paragraph is more nuanced and ambivalent, and concludes quite differently. Adams writes:

> Twenty times in the course of my late reading have I been on the point of breaking out, "This would be the best of all possible worlds if there were no religion in it!!" But in this exclamation I would have been fanatical. . . . Without religion, this world would be something not fit to be mentioned in polite company, I mean hell.[9]

Such a desire for a religionless world is "fanatical," and such a vision is "hell"? Adams, in the ordered comfort of eighteenth- and early nineteenth-century America, must have heard accounts of the French Revolution's bloodbath in the Vendée, which was the first great modern massacre in the name of secularism. But surely even his imagination would have been beggared by the monstrous horrors of the twentieth century, ranging from Stalin's terror famines in the Ukraine to Mao Zedong's utopian murderousness in the Cultural Revolution, to the killing fields of Pol Pot. For the blunt fact is that with the twentieth-century death toll under political repression at around 100 million, more people have been killed under secularist regimes, led by secularist intellectuals in the name of a secularist ideology, than in all the religious repressions and persecutions in Western history combined.

It will not do, as Christopher Hitchens often did, to excuse secularism by simply saying that all totalitarianism, even secularist totalitarianism, is essentially religious because it is totalitarian. That too is squaring the moral circle, though from the opposite direction. After the most murderous century in human history, secularists as well as religious believers have much to answer for. The crooked timber of our humanity is painfully obvious on all sides.

Soul freedom is for realists, not just idealists. It is urgent, not because humanity can be perfected through it but because without it the enduring flaws in the human condition will always exact a terrible price.

SEE IT RIGHT TO GET IT RIGHT

My purpose is not to play tit for tat, to point fingers or even to press for a more even-handed judgment. Refreshing though the latter would be, the stakes are far higher. That is, it is time to break with the stale and acrid arguments that leave the discussion of religion and secularism only at the level of a problem. Settling for scorched-earth warfare between "religionists" and "secularists," or between the straw man extremes of faith and reason, is a recipe for wrangling without end and disaster for us all.

There is more faith in reason and more reason in faith than the caricaturists will ever understand or admit. In any case, what the world needs is an acknowledgment of the inescapable necessity of our sources of meaning and belonging, a vision for how we might live constructively with the differences that stem from them, and a partnership between responsible secularists and responsible religious believers that could advance such a vision and lead to a decisive breakthrough for human relations in the global era.

This again is what this book is about. But the responsibility for that partnership rests with both sides, religious believers as well as secularists, and secularists no less than religious believers. In much of the Western world, secularists are dominant in the gate-keeping institutions, so no breakthrough will be possible without their cooperation. But many of us who seek to be thoughtful people of faith are reaching out to all who desire a better way for humankind, and we wait for a similar response from the community of thoughtful secularists.

I would wholeheartedly support what Jonathan Sacks calls a "great partnership" between religion and science and the proponents of each.[10] Science and religion are no more opposed than reason and faith. But regardless of these wider issues, the time has unquestionably come for thinking leaders and responsible citizens across the world to recognize the importance of the issues of soul freedom, civility and a civil public square, and address them with all the urgency they require. Our task is to lay the foundations for what could be history's first truly multifaith, international society of nations, and a genuinely new world order that is worthy of the global era.

Let us explore together the steps needed to secure soul freedom and to forge civility in the new global public square, an arena that could be a model and a pacesetter for civil public life for freedom-loving peoples throughout the world.

But this call to a grand revaluation challenges more than just religious and secularist leaders. It also challenges political and academic leaders across the world to face the fact that the present discussion of the "religious problem," which automatically links religion to fundamentalism, conflict, extremism and violence, and sees it only as atavistic, vestigial and pathological, is not only wrong but prejudiced and counterproductive. The religious issue is all that, but more too. It is far more than a lingering leftover from the premodern age. It is both more complicated and more crucial than that, for how we live with our deepest differences—over our core beliefs, including secularism—goes to the heart of the peril and the promise of our time.

Put differently, we need to see it right to get it right. The time has come for a monumental revaluation or paradigm shift in global thinking over the "religious issue." For too long, discussion of the issue has been handicapped in several critical ways. For a start, too many of the world's leaders have viewed the problem as only negative, and therefore left it at the domestic level for scholars to analyze, activists to fight and lawyers to defend, and at the international level for military strategists and security experts to counter.

In addition, many have limited their responses to the problem to academic reports, interfaith dialogues and citizen initiatives. And, finally, the highest political leaders have generally ducked the issue and left it to lesser leaders and ordinary citizens. The world now needs to move beyond such myopia, and move from the defensive to the constructive, from well-meaning religious visions to hard-nosed political solutions, and from the concern of ordinary citizens to the responsibility of the highest leaders.

Let me state plainly some of the separate issues that are at stake in the grand revaluation that we must undertake:

- The religious issue is more than a matter of societies *defending* themselves by countering violent extremism, essential though security issues are.

- At a higher level it is also a matter of *ordering* societies, in the midst of the exploding diversity of the global era, so that liberty, diversity and harmony can work for each other rather than against each other.

- At a higher level still it is even a matter of *revitalizing* societies through what we now understand as the wellsprings of civil society and social capital, and thus contributing to genuine human flourishing.

In other words, the world will be a better place only when we surmount the ignorance and prejudice that views freedom of religion and belief as solely for the religious, or that views it simply as a topic for foreign policy and a matter of Western nations standing for international human rights. Freedom of religion and belief is for all human beings, secularist as well as religious. And freedom of religion and belief must be established in Western public life as well as elsewhere. Failure to recognize this is a symptom of Western myopia and prejudice.

Yet once again there is no way around the difficulty of the challenge: the religious issue is uncomfortable for many people and troublesome to discuss without rising blood pressures. That is precisely because it is always left at the lowest level when it begs to be understood at more profound levels and in a richer way. The result of this discomfort is embarrassing. Many well-educated people are highly vocal experts about the wrongs of religion, but novices in knowing what to do about it.

Put the issue of soul freedom and civility in their widest context. One of the world's supreme but least discussed problems is the question of political governance in the global era, at a time when democratic politics is lagging far behind global communications and the spread of market capitalism. The grand issue is this: *How are we to promote global governance without a single world government, and so accomplish a truly multifaith and multicultural international society that is free, just and stable?* Establishing soul freedom, resolving the "religious problem" and creating the conditions for a civil and cosmopolitan global public square are essential prerequisites and key building blocks for the larger and longer-term challenges of global governance. But contrary to the first instincts of many who consider themselves liberals today, we can achieve genuine cosmopolitanism, not by opposing the logic of the religion but by embracing it in a truly liberal way.

Whatever faith or philosophy of life we each espouse, whether transcendental or naturalistic, consider the following argument as a whole. It presents a case for a major rethinking of a crucial global issue. It is time, and past time, to undertake a bold new initiative to address and resolve the problem of living with our deepest differences, and to help turn what is presently a dark negative in world affairs into a potential plus. Nothing less than that is the promise of soul freedom and civility in the global public square. It is for the good of all.

Again, it is time, and past time, to ponder the question. What does it say of us and our times that the Universal Declaration of Human Rights could not be passed today? And what does it say of the future of freedom of thought, conscience, religion and belief if it can be neglected and threatened even in the United States, where it once developed most fully—that it can be endangered anywhere? Who will step forward now to champion the cause of freedom for the good of all and for the future of humanity?

3

A WAR OF SPIRITS

THE SECOND STEP IN THE REVALUATION *is to appreciate*
that the religious and ideological situation in today's world raises
the challenge of living with our deepest differences to an unprece-
dented and urgent level that can only be ignored by putting the future
at risk.

If a map of the global religions looks like an untidy series of war
fronts, much of the domestic discussion in many countries appears
like a march through a minefield. At the same time, many Western
liberals are allergic to any mention of religion, while many conservatives react as equally allergic to any proposals for a change in the
way things have always been, as if all proposals for change were
utopian and dangerous. In addition, many stalwart defenders of
freedom of religion and belief have become so troubled by the constant betrayals of their rights in today's world that they despair of
any constructive society-wide solution, and see monitoring and
protesting as the only tasks left to them as they beat a slow and
heavy-hearted retreat. Anything other than protest and anything
less than all-out culture warring, they believe, is the coward's path
to appeasement.

Together, such attitudes spawn a deep suspicion of any positive proposal for soul freedom for all and a civil public square. To some, such notions are messy and unnecessary, to others they are naive and forlorn, and to others still they are disastrous and faithless. The trouble with such attitudes is that they are self-fulfilling. They leave the problem in the state it is in until, like an unattended wound, it grows gangrenous. Thus liberal critics often refuse to understand religion as it deserves, and so ensure that it never rises higher than a toxic problem. Similarly, many conservative critics refuse to examine the merits of constructive change, and so guarantee that the problems become intractable. Yet *intractable* is only the term we use for problems that no leader has had the courage to tackle, just as *realism* is widely used as an alibi for what is really a counsel of despair.

That said, the momentous scale of the challenge is undeniable, for living with our deepest differences has become a grand global issue in our time that many people do consider intractable. And as I keep insisting, this vision of soul freedom grows from realism about the human capacity for domination and enslavement as much as from idealism about the human capacity for freedom. Which means that the world cannot go forward without facing up to this dilemma, and no solution to the problem can succeed without doing justice to its immensity.

THE ADVANCE OF FREEDOM

There are three major factors creating the turbulence behind the problem and therefore the urgency of resolving it in our time. Together these factors raise issues for freedom of religion and belief that must be considered with great care—and immense courage. For the history of freedom demonstrates that advances in freedom are the fruit of hard-won victories over daunting challenges rather than armchair solutions dreamed up in easy times.

Such is the story of both freedom of speech and freedom of religion and belief. Five hundred years ago the Gutenberg press was the new technology of its time. It burst through earlier forms of social control and provoked the reaction that led to the age of the censor, the Index and the Inquisition. Not incidentally, the office of the first censor was created in Mainz in 1485, the city where Gutenberg lived and only thirty-five years after he had invented the printing press in 1450. But it was precisely these tyrannies over the mind that were challenged and overthrown in the name of freedom of speech.

In 1644, John Milton pitted truth against all such tyrannies when he wrote, "though all the winds of doctrine were let loose to play upon the earth, so Truth be in the field, we do injuriously by licensing and prohibiting to misdoubt her strength. Let her and falsehood grapple; who ever knew Truth put to the worse, in a free and open encounter?"[1] John Locke wrote similarly, forty-four years later, that truth

is not taught by laws, nor has she any need of force to procure her entrance into the minds of men. Errors indeed prevail by the assistance of foreign and borrowed succors. But if truth make not her own way into the understanding by her own light, she will be the weaker for any borrowed force violence can add to her.[2]

In the same way, it is a mistake to think that freedom of religion and belief rose, as so many imagine, in eighteenth-century Enlightenment salons over good wine, good conversations and a refined distaste for religion. In fact it rose in seventeenth-century churches and chapels, and in the anger and sorrow of religious believers outraged at the horrors of the European wars of religion and the troubled tensions that exploded into England's civil war.

Just so we must face up to the darkening challenges of our own day and use them as stepping-stones to advance toward a greater achievement of freedom for all rather than stumbling blocks to any action at all.

EVERYONE IS NOW EVERYWHERE

The new technologies and social media of our own day are raising serious issues for freedom, but more for freedom of speech rather than freedom of religion and belief. The first factor challenging freedom of religion and belief is the astonishing explosion of diversity of all kinds in the global era, including religious and ideological diversity. As modern people we are all more aware than ever before of "all those others" with all their differences, others who appear to confront us and call us into question at many turns in our daily lives. And the dilemma is far more than an expansion of little private religious preferences. Rather, ours is a world in which we find entire worldviews and ways of life elbow-to-elbow with other entire worldviews and ways of life, all within the same society, and all wishing to make their voices heard and to be taken seriously.

For a start, the decline of Western dominance and the crisis of Western identity and unity have unleashed a conflict of ideas and authorities that has embroiled the world for more than a hundred years. In 1795, in the last of his essays on history and progress, Immanuel Kant wrote famously "To Perpetual Peace." It was his vision of what it would take for Enlightenment leaders to ensure peace between the nations. Almost a hundred years later, in the opening words of his own last book, *Ecce Homo*, Friedrich Nietzsche predicted a very different future. All the power structures of the old world would be blown into the air. There would be convulsions, earthquakes, spasms and "wars such as there have never yet been on the earth." In the apocalyptic clash of ideas and powers, all politics would be absorbed into "a war of spirits."[3]

There is no question which of these two celebrated philosophers is closer to the mark today. The century since the last of them, with its two world wars and its clash of grand ideologies, has demonstrated the accuracy of Nietzsche's vision rather than that of Kant. Centuries'-old empires have collapsed and gone for good. Once-noble traditions have been left in ruins. Formerly solid certainties have evaporated into thin air. Existing power structures have been torn apart by power plays. And truths long considered advanced, assured and self-evident have dissolved into a confused welter of indeterminate claims, endless preferences and paralyzing options—and the war of spirits goes on.

But this is only the beginning. Add to it the social forces at work in the global era. Thanks to the effects of the media, travel, communications and the unprecedented migrations of peoples, we are now in a world where it is said with only a little exaggeration that "everyone is now everywhere." Periods such as first-century Rome can be cited as earlier precedents of a similar diversity, but globalization has made diversity a truly global phenomenon, and what social scientists call "pluralization" is now acknowledged to be a powerful feature of modern living, from consumer goods to sexual lifestyles to philosophies of life.

Even on top of this there is the further fact that the challenge of religious and ideological diversity is growing rather than shrinking. Ever since the Iranian revolution in 1979, it has become evident that we are in the midst of a massive religious resurgence that is sweeping the world, but one that this time is countered by a newly aggressive secularism. "God is back," the editor in chief and a colleague from the *Economist* announced in 2009 in direct contradiction of the celebrated "God is dead" headline from *Time* in 1966. But the essential evidence had then been on hand for three decades, and John Micklethwait and Adrian Wooldridge were cited as much for writing from a magazine and a country that famously didn't "do

God" than for offering startling new evidence.

"Why are so many unlikely people, including myself, suddenly talking about God?" asks Terry Eagleton, the acerbic, witty and sharp-penned literary critic and left-wing radical, in his excoriating attack on the new atheists.[4] Beyond question, the answer is that intelligent people are facing up to a worldwide resurgence of religion over the last thirty years that is stunning and incontrovertible.

The long-held Enlightenment presumption was that the mists of religion would disappear before the rising sun of reason, and thus the troublesome power of religion could be safely disarmed in one of three ways: by being consigned to the past, considered as only a problem, or confined to the private world. Yet quite the opposite has happened. In many parts of the world, religion has been revitalized, repoliticized and to some extent even reintellectualized. As the eminent sociologist Peter L. Berger has said famously, "Religion is as furiously alive as ever."[5]

Religion has been revitalized in the sense of both a growth in numbers and in intensity. It has been repoliticized in the sense that various expressions of resurgent religion speak and act as a public faith, and are no longer willing to be penned in to the private sphere. And to a significant degree certain faiths have also been reintellectualized in the sense that the case for faith is now made by many of the world's leading thinkers and philosophers. (As I write, for example, the new atheists find themselves strikingly outgunned in the latest exchanges with their critics, such as Terry Eagleton and Alvin Plantinga.)

What matters more than the facts of the resurgence is its significance. Today's resurgence of religion is not simply a restoration, for there is a new and unprecedented feature of the global configuration of religion in the modern world. We are seeing what Jose Casanova calls "the emerging dissociation of world religions, civilizational identities, and geopolitical territories."[6] In the cumbersome jargon of the academy, religions in the global era are increasingly becoming demonopolized, deconfessionalized and deterritorialized.

The novelty lies in the fact that religions are still decisively important, yet not in the way they used to be. On the one hand, the major world religions are increasingly becoming detached from the civilizational settings with which they have long been identified—Western Europeans and North and South Americans traditionally being Christian, Middle Easterners Muslim, Indians Hindu, South East Asians Buddhists, and so on. On the other hand, the major world religions are increasingly becoming global religions, with global claims and aspirations, and the result is a new form of "global denominationalism."[7]

This new interaction puts added weight, in its turn, on the purported "clash of civilizations," as Samuel Huntington famously expressed it. For as Casanova points out, the global situation makes the picture of the clash both illuminating and misleading. The "clash of civilizations" is illuminating because it throws light on the salience of religion in contemporary global affairs. But it is also misleading because "it still conceives of civilizations as territorial geopolitical units, akin to superpowers, having some world religion at its core."[8]

SHOOT FIRST, THINK AFTERWARD

Startling though the empirical realities are, acknowledging them is only the beginning. Yet it would be fair to say that the resurgence has caught many people off guard. It has triggered alarm rather than a careful assessment of its meaning, and the barely disguised disappointment of many intellectuals is clear in the vehemence and intolerance of their reactions. Indeed, wherever secularist thinking is strong, such as in Europe and among the educated classes around the world, some forms of secularism have come to pride themselves on their newly aggressive stance. In different countries there are different reasons for the widespread rage against religion that is palpable in certain circles today—in Ireland, it is a reaction against the sexual abuse scandals of the Catholic Church, in the United States a vehement rejection of the Christian right, and so on. But it is noticeable that many of today's new atheists rival old-line Marxists for their vehemence and their belligerent intolerance.

In short, far from taking place in a vacuum, the religious resurgence finds itself face to face with two equally aggressive forces, and the resulting clash creates much of the turbulence and danger of the present situation. On one side, the resurgence has been countered by a newly brutal repression, such as the Chinese persecution of the house church movement or the general repression of minorities such as the Baha'i and the Ahmadiyya in Muslim-majority countries. On the other side, the resurgence has been met by the newly aggressive Western secularism.

The resulting clash not only fuels further culture warring, but serves to exacerbate the violations of freedom of thought, conscience, religion and belief on both sides. Richard Dawkins, for example, is openly intolerant, embarrassingly so for many of his supporters, and has won for himself the label "fundamentalist secularist." The general reason lies in the way he makes no bones about his refusal to tolerate not only extremists but moderates who tolerate extremists. But he has also taken specific intolerant positions, such as his recommendation that the government should step in to prevent parents from "indoctrinating" their children into what he believes are the evils of religion.

Alarmism, antireligious intolerance or a more sophisticated distancing through the use of such categories as "extremism" and "fundamentalism" can all be a serious misreading of the situation. On the one hand, the resurgence of religion has implications for international dealings between nations, and it highlights realities that are essential to the analyses of any political leader or foreign policy realist. For from the perspective of those who prefer to take their faith neat, the loudly claimed benefits of Western freedom and market economics are easily mistaken for license and greed. The result is a serious deficiency in the soft-power persuasion of the West, which has to be made up through a reliance on hard-power strategies whose excesses are in danger of undermining the West in other ways. Indeed, to many observers in the world, Europe and the United States now stand under the judgment of their own abandoned ideals—as when the United States is better known for the abominable behavior of some of its troops and for such stubbornly defended practices as torture rather than for the nobler ideals of the American project.

On the other hand, the religious resurgence exposes some of the cultural contradictions at the heart of the advanced modern nations themselves. Recent trends in philosophy, such as postmodernism, not to speak of horrific earlier events such as the Nazi death camps, have already exposed the deficiencies of the Enlightenment vision of religionless progress, which was actually another name for the religion of progress.

Further, as many had warned earlier, when religious voices are denied their legitimate place and expression in social life, they can become explosively antisocial. Over the centuries many of Europe's own social revolutionaries, from the late-medieval millenarians to the eighteenth-century Jacobins, to the twentieth-century Marxists, have had apocalyptic visions that were essentially religious, whatever their secularist pretensions—differing only in their respective visions of "the Day of the Lord" that was to come, and the different political means through which "the arm of the Lord" would be revealed.[9] No thinking Westerner should therefore have been taken by surprise at the religious dimension of anti-Western reactions today, whether avowedly secular, such as postcolonial nationalism, or openly religious, such as Islamist terrorism.

In sum, the combination of the Western lack of faith and the Western lack of understanding of faiths renders the West clumsily incompetent when face to face with the raging faiths on steroids in other parts of the world. It therefore raises the question of the enduring place of religion in human affairs and exposes an underlying instability in the West itself. For sickly faiths and shrinking ethical norms have no strength to provide the West the identity and unity they once had. Nor do they have the ability to guide, check and balance such powerful forces as Western freedom, capitalism, science, technology and consumerism.

The result is the unsurprising crisis of Western identity and the unaccountable permissiveness, the unfettered market forces, the unbounded moral and cultural relativism, the unashamed political pragmatism, the unchallenged philosophical skepticism, and the unchecked scientism that characterize the West today and that work together to undermine the ideals that have made the West the civilization it once was.

In short, everyone is now everywhere, and in ways that can be volatile and explosive.

THE MORPHING OF THE PUBLIC SQUARE

The second factor creating turbulence concerns a key development in the notion of the public square, which has morphed to a new level that is raising new problems. Ever since the golden age of Greece, the idea of the public square has been precious and important to all who prize democracy and democratic freedoms. At the outset, the public square was a physical place, the *agora* in Athens down below the Acropolis and the Areopagus, and later the forum in Rome. In each city it was far more than the marketplace and even "the marketplace of ideas," as the term is commonly translated today when economics is dominant. The public square was the civic center of the state, the physical place where citizens came together to deliberate and decide issues of common public life. In that sense the term still describes certain physical places today, such as the Houses of Parliament at Westminster, the French National Assembly and the United States Congress.

But over time, and especially in the English-speaking democracies, the notion of the public square came to be seen as wider than these official places. It was the metaphor also used of other forums that were neither formal nor official, but also were part of the public square, such as the op-ed pages of the newspapers and the talk shows on radio and television. Today, however, the public square has morphed again through the power of the Internet, and has gone from the physical to the metaphorical to the virtual. There are many lessons to be learned from the responses to Salman Rushdie's novel *The Satanic Verses* in 1989, the Danish cartoons depicting the Prophet Muhammad in 2005, Pope Benedict XVI's speech at the University of Regensburg in 2006, and the anti-Islamic video "Innocence of Muslims" that roiled much of the Muslim world in 2012. But chief among them is the simple fact that *even when we are not speaking to the world, we can be heard by the world, and the world can organize its response as never before. The whole world can now talk back to the whole world.*

Beyond question there are pluses and minuses in the impact of the new social media. Most of them go far beyond our topic here, though suffice it to say that the single strongest benefit is the new capacity it gives individuals to be active and interactive rather than passive. We are therefore seeing the emergence of new forums for discussing public affairs, such as Facebook, Twitter, blogs, webinars and a host of new technological wonders such as SADNs ("self-assembling dynamic networks")—as seen in recent events as diverse as the Arab Spring and the Occupy Wall Street protests. In short, we are beginning to see the very real if rudimentary outlines of a global public square in which the affairs of the world are being debated urgently and passionately around the world.

Beyond question there are minuses too, for the increase in the ease, speed and number of participants in the communication has not been matched by a similar increase in the quality of the thinking and the civility of the debates. Are we then to resign ourselves to present levels of incivility, to debates and decisions based on fifteen-second sound bites, 140-character tweeted arguments, degrading rhetoric from masked attackers with anonymous screen names, and the dubious viral capacity to whip up instant protests and flash mobs? Or can we in the next twenty-five years forge a new understanding of what it means for global citizens to debate other global citizens in a manner that the issues deserve, and one that is worthy of the democratic heritage of which we are the heirs? Such are some of the practical spinoffs of the challenges of living with our deepest differences, and it is in the face of such stubborn and messy realities that we have to consider what it means to establish soul freedom and civility in the global public square and to sustain a free, democratic and responsible world citizenry.

OLD SETTLEMENTS FLOUNDERING

The third factor creating turbulence stems from the fact that many of the world's traditional settlements of religion and public life are floundering. Forged under the conditions of an earlier day, they are proving inadequate to the demands of freedom and justice in an age of exploding diversity. They therefore need to be renegotiated with care under the conditions of today, though many of their defenders instinctively close their eyes to all questions of change and insist on pressing the merits of their long-held systems, oblivious to the shortcomings that have recently been exposed.

Following the Reformation and the great division of Christendom in the sixteenth century, much of Europe lived under the Westphalian settlement whereby *cuius regio, eius religio* (as your ruler, so your religion). This in turn led to the more modern settlements of religion and public life—of which the French, the English and the American are among the most prominent. Each of these was forged at a key moment in its nation's history and in response to specific historical circumstances—the English settlement in the Glorious Revolution of 1688, the French in the revolution of 1789, and the American at the time of the First Amendment to the Bill of Rights in 1791. Supporters of each can cite the strong merits of their respective settlements, both at the time of its devising and for many years afterward.

For the English the 1628 Petition of Right, the Bill of Rights and the Toleration Act of 1689 and the continued establishment of the Church of England were designed to expand a limited freedom for the new Christian diversity, to match the benefits of the growing Dutch toleration and to provide a Protestant bulwark to counter the threats seen as coming from across the Channel in Catholic France.

For the French the strict *laicité* of the Jacobin radicals after 1789 was designed to remedy the corruption and oppression of the pre-revolutionary church and state, and to promote the interests of the growing Enlightenment atheism.

And for Americans the 1791 settlement effected by America's First Amendment to the Bill of Rights was designed to protect religious liberty by separating church and state, but not religion and public life—thus making religion voluntary, and by doing so allowing all religions to flourish, not despite disestablishment but because of it.

Yet regardless of the pros and cons of each settlement, they are all clearly under severe stress today and need to be readjusted significantly in light of current conditions and especially the worldwide explosion of diversity.

Much of what remains of the Anglican establishment in England is notoriously weak, spiritually, numerically and culturally, and has suffered recently from amiable but confusing leadership. It is therefore struggling to stand up to what Bishop Michael Nazir-Ali calls the "triple jeopardy" facing the West—an aggressive secularism, a radical Islamism and multiculturalism.[10] Unless the Church recovers its integrity and effectiveness, it will lose even more authority in the country and may soon face involuntary disestablishment.

Thus, when faced with the unprecedented immigration of the 1970s, the British (along with the Dutch) fell back on their historically prized default position of tolerance. And in the name of tolerance they responded to the immigration with the reigning ideology of tolerance of the day—state multiculturalism—and inadvertently encouraged the building of the religious enclaves that failed to integrate the new immigrants and literally blew up in their faces in the 7/7 bombings of July 7, 2005, and the murder of the film director Theo van Gogh. Avoiding assimilation at all costs, they produced something worse, alienation, and were left to rue the consequences of their confusion.

England's present muddle and its lack of a civil public square is captured perfectly in the case of the women forbidden to wear a cross at their government workplace and told by government lawyers that they should "leave their beliefs at home or get another job."[11] The cross is the chief symbol of the Christian faith, and in the form of the Church of England the Christian faith remains the official faith of the nation. Yet the women were banned from wearing the symbol of the established faith of the land, and in their appeal to the European courts they were opposed by their own government's lawyers and left undefended by their own archbishop at the time, who described the cross as only a decoration. Decoration? In one sense, yes, of course. But in another, it has been the most decisive symbol in all history, for better or worse, as Roman Catholic and Evangelical leaders were far quicker to make clear.

Religious establishment versus new state orthodoxy? Where are *Punch* and Malcolm Muggeridge when we need them? Only a seasoned humorist could capture the comic contortions of the English today. As one MP expressed it, "The Prime Minister made it plain in the House of Commons that the Government believes that the wearing of religious symbols in the workplace is a vital freedom. One therefore has to ask why the Government's lawyers are the last to know."[12]

The strict *laïcité* of the French settlement has experienced similar but more straightforward pressures. A far cry from the tolerance of the Edict of Nantes, it owes its origins to the French Revolution and the violent disgust at the result of Louis XIV's revocation of the Edict of Nantes. The Jacobin radicals sought to fulfill Diderot's maxim and "strangle the last king with the guts of the last priest." Their understandable response to a church and a state that were both corrupt and oppressive was to throw out both. This naturally cemented the mentality, powerful in France ever since, that if you were in favor of faith, you must be reactionary, and if you were in favor of freedom, you must be secular. The result of course has been an ever-stricter separation of religion and public life that favors secularism, but does no justice to the recent arrival in France of rapidly growing religious populations, especially from Muslim lands.

The American settlement was the most revolutionary in its time, reversing fifteen hundred years of European church-state arrangements. In his "Memorial and Remonstrance," James Madison hailed it as the "true remedy" for the age-old problems of religion and public life, and for nearly two hundred years it was arguably the most nearly perfect solution so far to the problems that had plagued the world for centuries. Today, however, fifty years of culture warring illustrate how far America has drifted from its founders' solutions, for Americans have reduced their public life to a war zone of cultural controversies with all the attendant ugliness of bitterness, litigiousness, polarizations and gridlock—a "war of spirits" if ever there was one.

It could be argued that neither the English nor the French settlements are fully suited to the explosively diverse conditions of the advanced modern global era, and require a more radical renegotiation. But there is a special poignancy in the failure of the American settlement. For in the fractiousness of their recent public controversies, Americans are failing to live up to the pioneering success of their founding generation. They are therefore failing to model to the world a solution that still carries immense and unfulfilled potential if it were understood better and followed more consistently. Madison's own country is no longer applying his "true remedy," and the unhealthy symptoms he feared are breaking out again.

Few Americans seem to appreciate an irony that is glaring from the outside. The United States hailed itself from the beginning as Livy's *novus ordo seclorum* (new order of the ages), and later as the world's "first new nation"—both for good reasons. Yet when these claims were first made, the rest of the world shrugged their shoulders and went on their ancient ways, unimpressed. No other countries at the time were facing the social and political conditions that made the American experiment so audacious and its early success so revolutionary.

Today in the global era, however, much of the globalizing world is convulsed by the same challenges that the United States first faced more than two centuries ago—massive immigration and exploding religious diversity, for example. Thus the vital significance of the success of the American experiment, and the lessons of particular accomplishments such as the First Amendment and the Melting Pot are now, for the first time, urgent for the whole world.

But at the very moment when America could truly have a chance of being a "city on a hill" and a shining example to the world, America has gone AWOL. From being the great pioneer and pacesetter of religious freedom, the United States is rapidly degenerating into becoming another example of the problem. Far from living up to the promise of its past, America is heedlessly indulging in acrimonious culture warring as if its past had never happened and it were any other nation emerging late into the unforgiving conditions of modernity. And to this point no national leader has broken ranks with the culture warriors to point to a better way.

Be that as it may, much of the world now finds itself where the United States has been for more than two hundred years. America's motto, *E pluribus unum*, is now echoed directly by the slogan of the European Union widely plastered across Brussels: "United in diversity." And the kaleidoscopic diversity it refers to is the challenge of more countries across the world than ever before, including the emerging new powers China and India, which both represent a remarkable diversity of faiths and a challenge to their governments. How then do we live with our deepest differences so that diversity and harmony are able to complement rather than contradict each other? What America faced two hundred years ago, the whole world faces today.

The American founders are commonly dismissed or accused of hypocrisy because of the contradiction between their ringing declarations of freedom and their treatment of slaves, women and Native Americans. Beyond any doubt, the accusation is just when it comes to those issues, and such founders as Thomas Jefferson are shown up as the rank hypocrites they were. But at the same time, the American founders got freedom of thought and conscience right, almost from the very start, and the lessons of their high achievement in this area must not be lost in the general rush to judge their other failings.

To America's credit *E pluribus unum* is not only its national motto but its greatest achievement. That same task now faces the world. Put these three factors together, and we can feel the urgency of why living with our deepest differences has become a global problem, which needs to have a global solution. The place to begin is with a comprehensive and sober assessment of why the challenge is central and unavoidable today.

Again, it is time, and past time, to ponder the question. What does it say of us and our times that the Universal Declaration of Human Rights could not be passed today? And what does it say of the future of freedom of thought, conscience, religion and belief if it can be neglected and threatened even in the United States, where it once developed most fully—that it can be endangered anywhere? Who will step forward now to champion the cause of freedom for the good of all and for the future of humanity?

4

FIRST
FREEDOM FIRST

THE THIRD STEP IN THE REVALUATION *is to restore the primacy and high priority of establishing freedom of thought, conscience, religion and belief for people of all faiths and none, both for the sake of individual human persons and for the common good of humanity itself.*

Why freedom of thought, conscience, religion and belief? Consider one of the key periods in the story of human rights: the American Revolution and the unique American settlement of religion and public life. This period is important because it was the time when this foundational freedom passed from being the passionate concern of individuals and groups fighting against different oppressions to being the concern of statesmen and the architects who desired to build it into free and open societies. A striking feature of this period was the way the founders of the United States repeatedly twinned the two notions of religious liberty and civil liberty. Again and again, in both their speeches and their writings, they saw the two rights as the twin brothers of freedom, neither of which could prevail without the other.

But at the same time, the American founders clearly held that soul freedom, or freedom of thought, conscience, religion and belief, was the "first liberty." For one thing, it grew from the first of the three foundational political rights: freedom of conscience, freedom of speech or expression, and freedom of assembly or association. For another, and this is a crucial point today, soul freedom was inherent in the very notion of humanity and therefore a right for all humans as humans, whereas a civil right is inherent only in the citizenship of those whose political agreements and arrangements make it a reality.

When freedom of religion and belief has been seen rightly, it has not only been regarded as the first liberty but as the litmus test for assessing the conditions of other freedoms too. This is why it is a grave concern that freedom of religion and belief is under such a cloud today. In what is becoming an open affront to all human rights, civil liberty is increasingly preferred to freedom of religion and belief, and when the two clash, freedom of religion and belief has even been dismissed as an obstruction—as if it were not a right at all. This is partly due to a specific tactic of certain activists we will examine later, and partly due to the general point I have already underscored: that a striking feature of the contemporary world is that, to the degree that religion is under a cloud in educated circles, so also is freedom of religion and belief. The latter's stock has fallen along with former in the university stock market of ideas. Religion is dismissed as subjective, irrational and toxic, and what was once the first liberty guarding it is now often the first to be abandoned or at least downgraded as overrated and unnecessary. Far from its ranking as the first liberty, freedom of religion and belief has become one of the most neglected and embattled of human rights.

CUT-FLOWER CIVILIZATION

The willful neglect of this foundational freedom is a serious problem, and unless it is addressed, it will prove consequential to the future of free and open societies. But it has been compounded by an even deeper problem. The Western world, which has been the pioneer and champion of the human rights revolution, is experiencing a grand moral and philosophical confusion over how human rights are to be grounded and justified at all. At first glance it would seem that human rights need no grounding. Cited on all sides and on a thousand occasions, they are today's self-evident truths to many people—as obvious and logical as two plus two makes four, as powerful as belief in God in the great ages of faith, and the instinctive resort of all who face injustice or feel hard done by. Indeed, the human rights revolution has become for many a religion in itself.

But that blind belief is naive. Human rights can no more be taken for granted today than belief in God in a senior common room in a modern university. Take the three core notions that many modern people still consider self-evident and unassailable: human dignity, liberty and equality. Along with a whole range of beliefs in the modern world, there is confusion as to how they are to be understood and a yawning chasm as to how they are to be grounded. Originally pioneered in the West and grounded in Jewish and Christian beliefs, human dignity, liberty and equality are now often left hanging without agreement over their definition and their foundation.

There is a cold logic to the present quandary. If the original Jewish and Christian foundations of human dignity, liberty and equality are to be rejected, the ideas themselves need to be transposed to a new key or eventually they will wither. The Western world now stands as a cut-flower civilization, and such once-vital convictions have a seriously shortened life.

Without healthy roots for human dignity, for example, liberty and equality will eventually wither too. That outcome is as certain as any mathematical certainty. Jefferson was no champion of religion, but in his *Notes on the State of Virginia*, he stated his conviction firmly: "God who gave us life gave us liberty. And can the liberties of a nation be thought secure when we have removed their only firm basis, a conviction in the minds of the people that these liberties are the Gift of God?"[1] John F. Kennedy, a nominal Catholic, was not religiously devout either and was described by some of his friends as a humanist. But as late as 1961 he could state in his inaugural address what was clearly unobjectionable to a liberal of half a century ago, "The rights of man come not from the generosity of the state but from the hand of God."[2]

Nietzsche himself was insistent on the logic of the cut flowers as befits a man who set out to do philosophy with a hammer. If indeed contemporary society deems that God is dead, then sooner or later all that God was once responsible for will go too. We cannot have it both ways, the great iconoclast argued. We cannot unhinge the sun and wipe away the horizon and expect everything to stay the same and the world go on as before. There may be a lag between the lightning and the thunder, but the storm will come. Or in C. S. Lewis's homelier illustration, to think otherwise is to repeat the folly of the woman in the Second World War who said she was not bothered by the threatened bread shortage because her family ate toast.

Thanks to the seismic cultural effects of the 1960s and especially of postmodernism, there is now a greater gap over the grounding of Western convictions between the present generation and 1960 than between 1776 and 1960. Postmodern philosophers such as Richard Rorty have even argued for abandoning all attempts to ground human rights on sure foundations ("the emergence of human rights culture seems to owe nothing to increased moral knowledge, and everything to hearing sad and sentimental stories").[3] Today, there is such confusion surrounding human dignity, liberty and equality that they are being called into question as incoherent, insubstantial and unsustainable—incoherent because of the lack of agreement in the differing accounts, insubstantial because all three notions are still vigorously asserted despite the glaring absence of any apparent foundation for their claims, and unsustainable because even their supporters rarely seem to offer any consideration as to how they are to be maintained in the face of growing worldwide pressures against them.

Severed roots are not the sum of the problem for human rights. They are equally threatened from an entirely different angle by the trivialization that has followed the popularity of rights and rights language. As Milan Kundera has protested, "the more the fight for human rights gains in popularity the more it loses any concrete content, becoming a kind of universal stance of everyone towards everything, a kind of energy that turns all human desires into rights. The world has become man's right and everything in it has become a right."[4] Thus every desire morphs into a right—currently, the desire to love is swelling into the right to love—and everything that is a matter of human decency sooner or later is held to be a basic and inviolable right—such as a child's "right to play" and so on.

As with the inflation of easily printed money, when more is available, less and less is valuable. Thus the more rights we promote, the more they will clash. But worse still, the more rights we promote, the less they will mean, so that steadily expanding rights will bring steadily diminishing returns. Far better the few, the precious and the foundational than the many and the meaningless.

Clarifying all this confusion will be critical to the future of free societies, as anyone can attest who knows the degrading anthropologies of Stalin's Russia, Hitler's Germany and Mao's China. In the end, such a change of worldviews will mean decisive changes for the understanding of humanity, for the defense of human rights and ultimately for the treatment of human beings. Just as the road to Auschwitz began in professors' studies and academic lecture halls, so the present degraded views of humanity will inevitably create a harvest of evil consequences, even if not fully visible now.

FAITH MUST BE VOLUNTARY

We therefore need to ground and justify all such self-evident notions as human dignity, liberty and equality, for in today's setting nothing is self-evident. In particular, we need to remind ourselves why freedom of thought, conscience, religion and belief is so important, why the early pioneers of soul freedom saw it as integral to freedom and indispensable to a free and just society, and why it is that every charter of human rights includes the right to freedom of thought, conscience, religion and belief as an essential.

Freedom of speech is more fashionable today than freedom of religion and belief, but freedom of speech is no longer self-evident either. It needs to be justified again and again in every generation (as an expression of human dignity, as an essential of self-governance and as a key to the free market of ideas). Not surprisingly, then, freedom of religion and belief requires fresh justification too, and there are solid and sufficient reasons to do so—reasons that in turn form a key part of the wider reaffirmation and justification of freedom itself.

To be sure, each individual faith that prizes freedom of religion and belief is responsible to advance its own internal reasons for justifying it. The Abrahamic faiths, for example, have all argued (and all too often not practiced what they preached) that God has no interest in faith that is coerced. Coercion and consent are a contradiction in terms. The commitment that is the act of trust in God is essentially and necessarily free and fully responsible. Rousseau's notion of being "forced to be free," which he argued in *The Social Contract*, is an oxymoron that has no place in the Jewish and Christian faiths ("Whoever refuses to obey the general will shall be compelled to it by the whole body: this in fact only forces him to be free").

Neither thinking itself nor any warranted beliefs are ever subject to the will alone, so freedom of conscience stems from the recognition that no person can demand of another what the other simply cannot do as a matter of will alone. An implication of the traditional notion of hell is that even God refuses to override the settled convictions of our human freedom and responsibility. We are never forced to be free.

From this Jewish and Christian perspective, freedom of thought, conscience, religion and belief matters because faith, to be true to itself and faithful to God, must be free and uncoerced. It must be voluntary. Needless to say, however strong such arguments are, they can be dismissed as self-serving and unique to each faith, when what matters are the reasons for freedom of religion and belief that are common to all humanity. These too are strong.

The Freedom to Be Human

Powerful logical and historical arguments have been advanced as to why freedom of religion and belief is the first liberty, and I will mention them later. But there is an even stronger prior argument that must be acknowledged. First and foremost, freedom of thought, conscience, religion and belief is important because it is the direct expression and the deepest protection of our freedom and responsibility to be human. *Freedom of religion and belief affirms the dignity, worth and agency of every human person by freeing us to align "who we understand ourselves to be" with "what we believe ultimately is," and then to think, live, speak and act in line with those convictions.* Nothing comes closer to the heart of our humanity than the self-understanding and the self-constitution made possible through freedom of thought, conscience, religion and belief. As a right, it is primary, foundational and indispensable.

Conscience is the inner forum of an individual person, in which the grand debates about reality and unreality, truth and falsehood, right and wrong are finally settled for each of us. So what the freedom of a public square is to a city or a nation, freedom of conscience is to a person. Respect these twin forums together, one inner and one outer, and do so for people of all faiths, and you create a fair, open and profoundly human community.

There are important qualifications to this right—above all the equal rights of others, as well as consideration for the public peace and the common good. Or put differently, this freedom is absolute at the point of belief but qualified at the point of behavior, because behavior touches other people and other things. Someone is free to believe in paganism, for example, but not to sacrifice an animal or another human being.

But that said, the primary and foundational character of the right must never be lost. Philosopher Christopher Tollefsen makes the point simply and elegantly: "Judgments of conscience are our final verdict on how we are to constitute ourselves. Such judgments are thus an exercise of one of the two capacities jointly necessary for our being active self-constituters; the other is our capacity for freedom, a capacity exercised in our choices to act as consciences dictates."[5]

The right to freedom of thought, conscience, religion and belief speaks to the heart of our humanness, just as our humanness flowers most fully in this freedom. It is of course a promise that must be cashed in, a possibility that must be turned into an opportunity. As such, it is nothing less than what Tollefsen calls "the capacity for realized personhood."[6]

Can freedom flourish if the twin forums are not respected, and the free exercise of freedom is systematically curtailed? Can freedom last for a people who have no foundation for a high view of human worth? Always a theoretical question, the latter has become a practical, burning issue today, for current views of humanity are steadily degrading human worth and are unable to restore it to its former place. Yet the lesson for liberal societies is stark: Abandon or lose our conviction of human dignity and the day will come when we have no liberty or equality either.

Article 1 of the Global Charter of Conscience affirms:

> Freedom of thought, conscience, and religion, which together may be described as religious freedom, is a precious, fundamental, and inalienable human right—the right to adopt, hold, freely exercise, share, or change one's beliefs, subject solely to the dictates of conscience and independent of all outside, especially governmental control. This freedom includes all ultimate beliefs and worldviews, whether supernatural or secular, transcendent or naturalistic.

Soul liberty was Roger Williams's stirring seventeenth-century term for the freedom of thought, conscience and religion for which he fought.[7] Williams was well schooled in common law and by an uncommon lawyer, Sir Edward Coke, who was England's greatest jurist and champion of freedom. Coke had defied James I's claim to the divine right of kings, and had gone to the Tower of London for his stand on Magna Carta and what he considered the ancient liberties of the English.

Williams and his fellow pioneers of freedom of thought and conscience regarded this right as inherent, not only in common law but in the very nature of humanity and the human family. It was rooted in the inviolable dignity of each human person and in particular in the character of reason and conscience, the twin organs of thinking and moral intuitions. For Williams and others later, such as John Milton and John Locke, these ideas in their turn were rooted in the conviction that humans possessed this dignity because they were made in the image of God.

What Magna Carta was to the ancient liberties of the English, being made in the image of God is for all human beings. Each human has a measureless worth that goes beyond any possible descriptions of status, function and utility. All other descriptions are vulnerable to our being reduced to our functions and utilitarian qualities—we are made less when we are merely voters or viewers or buyers or consumers or passengers or statistics and so on. But made in the image of God, we each possess an equal and inalienable worth that is prior to every other category and consideration. This dignity and worth is therefore inalienable and inviolable.

The alternatives to this high view of human dignity are starkly different, and as so often, differences make a difference—for example, views such as the ethicist Peter Singer's that demean humans to the level of animals or such as Jean Jacques Rousseau's that regard human rights as the gift of the state and merely a result of the social contract that underlies all human society. "The State, in relation to its members, is master of all their goods by the social contract, which, within the State, is the basis of all their rights."[8] The result of such views, as night follows day, is that the will of the individual must always bow to the general will, and the individual person to the collective. No rights are therefore inviolable and inalienable in themselves but merely a grant and favor of society.

Over against the deficient views of Rousseau, whose logic flowers naturally but most fully and foully in totalitarianism and a denial of all human rights, it was once held firmly in the West that every human had dignity and worth. It is therefore the right of every human to inquire into the nature of reality, to form his or her own convictions of what is true, and to live according to the consequences of those ultimate beliefs and thus according to the dictates of conscience. Such a right is a matter of universal justice as well as freedom, or a matter of freedom and a universal right because it is a matter of justice. There is a common link running between foundational convictions, such as human dignity, and such notions as the "good life" and the "examined life": every human has the duty and the right to reach and hold his or her own convictions about the nature of reality, the meaning life and the grounds of right and wrong—and those convictions, or ultimate beliefs, are inalienable and inviolable.

What true liberal or what freedom-loving conservative can argue with each person's right to think and order his or her life in accordance with what he or she believes to be true, based on the dictates of conscience? To be sure, it will have to be decided how the freedom this right gives to each person is to relate to the equal freedom of all others, to the public peace and to the common good. But it anchors the principle that what needs to be negotiated is an absolute right, and not merely a matter of tolerance, let alone the luxury of a social privilege conferred by the state.

To be sure, some have tried to relativize liberty of thought, conscience, religion and belief. They argue that it can be viewed historically as the accomplishment of some that has become the aspiration of others, or as the achievement of the religious that is irrelevant to the secular. But that is to confuse the recognition of the right with the right itself. At a deeper level that we must never allow to be obscured, the freedom and the right are absolute and not relative. They are inherent in humanity itself and in every individual human person rather than simply in citizenship and the membership of some political community. As Lord Acton declared simply, "By birth all men are free."[9]

This insistence on the birthright of human belonging is vital for another reason. It points beyond individualism and the danger of rights becoming a form of selfish claims to entitlement. Freedom of thought, conscience, religion and belief is always individual in the sense that it truly covers every last one of us, with no one ever excepted. But at the same time, it is never solitary or individualistic.

It is an individual right that is a matter of membership, the birthright of belonging to the human family, and the equal right of every human being regardless of religion, gender, race, class, language, political or other opinion, or nationality, and regardless of any mental and physical handicap and any social, economic or educational deprivation. Without this rich understanding and protection of freedom of thought, conscience and religion, we cannot do justice to our humanity as individual persons or as members of communities, nor to our lives whether lived in private or in public.

In the powerful words of Timothy Samuel Shah:

> Anything less than full religious freedom fails to respect the dignity of persons as free truth-seekers, duty bound to respond to the truth (and only the truth) about the transcendent in accordance with their own judgments of conscience. . . . When people lose their religious freedom, they lose more than their freedom to be religious. They lose their freedom to be human.[10]

A CLOSED ACCORDION PLAYS NO MUSIC

By the same token, freedom of thought, conscience, religion and belief does not stand alone, and it must always be understood in its relationships to other members of the family of rights. Externally, it is part and parcel of the three core political rights: freedom of conscience, freedom of expression and freedom of association. Internally, it covers a range of different freedoms: variously described as covering "the right to explore, to embrace, and to express" or the right to "profess, to practice, and to propagate."

Like an accordion expanding or contracting to make music, this range of rights can sometimes be squeezed down and summed up tersely as "freedom of thought, conscience, religion and belief." But again like an accordion, its full range can best be appreciated when it is expanded to include the notes of all the rights—"the right to adopt, hold, freely exercise, share, or change one's beliefs, subject solely to the dictates of conscience and independent of all outside, especially governmental control." *And again, this freedom must of course be promoted and protected for people of all faiths, religious, nonreligious or anti-religious.*

In today's world, it has grown difficult to grasp the rich fullness and complexity of religious freedom. Such is the radioactive climate of the contemporary culture wars that all that seems to survive is the stunted speech of slogans, stereotypes, stick figures and slanders—rather than the luxuriant health of discourse in freer and more tolerant times. But the full complexity of religion that is guarded by freedom of religion and belief must be remembered, and constitutional scholar Michael W. McConnell expresses it admirably:

> Religion is a special phenomenon, in part, because it plays such a wide variety of roles in human life: it is an institution, but it is more than that; it is an ideology or worldview, but it is more than that; it is a set of personal loyalties and locus of community, akin to family ties, but it is more than that; it is an aspect of identity, but is more than that; it provides questions of ultimate reality, and it offers connections to the transcendent; but it is more than that. Religion cannot be reduced to a subset of any larger category.[11]

It is this rich, full understanding that makes soul freedom for all so revolutionary and the society that practices it so genuinely open and free. Few understand this fact today, whether new world powers, such as China, wrestling with old problems, or old powers, such as Europe, wrestling with new problems, and even Americans for whom fifty years of culture-warring has fatally distanced them from their roots. For the fact is that there was nothing, absolutely nothing, in the entire American experiment more revolutionary, unique and decisive than the first sixteen words of the First Amendment to the Bill of Rights, the two famous religious liberty clauses that together stand guard over this right ("Congress shall make no law respecting an establishment of religion, or prohibiting the free exercise thereof").

At one stroke, what Marx later called "the flowers on the chains" and Lord Acton the "gilded crutch of absolutism"was stripped away.[12] The persecution that Williams called "spiritual rape" and a "soul yoke," and Lord Acton called "spiritual murder," was prohibited. The burden of centuries of oppression was lifted, what Williams lamented as "the rivers of civil blood" spilled by faulty relations between religion and government were staunched, and faith was put on its free and fundamental human footing as "soul liberty"—Williams's term for what was a matter of individual conscience and uncoerced freedom.

The Williamsburg Charter, a celebration of the genius of the First Amendment on the occasion of its two hundredth anniversary, summarized the public aspect of this stunning achievement:

> No longer can sword, purse, and sacred mantle be equated. Now, the government is barred from using religion's mantle to become a confessional State, and from allowing religion to use the government's sword and purse to become a coercing Church. In this new order, the freedom of the government from religious control and the freedom of religion from government control are a double guarantee of the protection of rights. No faith is preferred or prohibited, for where there is no state-definable orthodoxy, there can be no state-definable heresy.[13]

America's First Amendment was of course no bolt out of the blue. It was a high peak, but only one such on the long, slow, tortuous road to religious freedom that can be traced all the way back to early Christian thinkers. Tertullian, from Carthage, was the very first to use the term "religious freedom" (*libertas religionis*). He wrote, "It is a fundamental human right, a privilege of nature, that every man should worship according to his own convictions."[14] Jefferson actually owned a copy of this third-century book, and had underlined these words. A century later they were echoed by another Christian apologist, Lactantius, who tutored Constantine's son. Such thinking, then, was behind the co-emperors' famous Edict of Milan (A.D. 313), which was the first official state document to set out the principle of religious freedom.

Despite such ancient and auspicious beginnings, religious freedom had long been neglected, and its rise in the modern world grew more directly out of revulsion to corrupt state churches, reactions to the horrors of the Wars of Religion and the daring bravery of thinkers such as Thomas Hywels, Roger Williams, Henry Robinson, William Penn, John Leland, Isaac Backus, George Mason, Thomas Jefferson, James Madison, the Culpeper Baptists and many others.

Many of these champions of soul freedom, such as Roger Williams and William Penn, were Englishmen. But sadly for the English, the seeds of the freedom that had been sown in England never came to full flower in their homeland, and today they are menaced more than ever. So it is beyond question that many of the great peaks of the story and many of the greatest heroes lie in the terrain of American history. In the great "argument between friends," for example, the maverick dissenter Roger Williams clashed with the orthodox John Cotton of Boston in challenging the notion of "the uniformity of religion in a civil state" and the "doctrine of persecution" that had inevitably accompanied it in European history and throughout the world (before him and in our own time).

This pernicious doctrine, Williams thundered, "is proved guilty of all the blood of the souls crying for vengeance under the altar."

In its place, he asserted, "it is the will and command of God that . . .
*a permission of the most paganish, Jewish, Turkish, or anti-Christian
consciences and worships* be granted to all men in all nations and
countries, and they are only to be fought against with that sword
which is only, in soul matters, able to conquer, to wit, the sword of
God's Spirit, the word of God."[15]

Soul freedom, in short, is not for some but for all. No government and no authority must ever come between citizens and
their conscience, and their conscience itself must be won only
through persuasion and never coercion. Anything else, Williams
declared, is a "molesting" of conscience and a "rape" of the soul.

More than a century after Williams, James Madison rang out the
same themes in his "Memorial and Remonstrance," almost like an
echo of Williams. He was protesting against Patrick Henry's proposal to levy a religion tax that everybody could earmark for the
church of their choice. No, the little man with the quiet voice protested, hammering home point after point with precision as well as
force, this was absolutely wrong and there was a better way.

TIME TO WALK THE TALK

Is such a defense and all such talk of freedom merely what Walter
Bagehot famously dismissed as "historic twaddle about the rise of
liberty," or Jeremy Bentham ridiculed earlier as "nonsense upon
stilts"?[16] All too easily it can be, and it is important to see the main
ways in which this vital freedom to be human can be undermined.

- First, it can be destroyed by deficient views of humanity that
  give no grounds for the possibility of judgments of conscience.

- Second, it can be damaged by blocking or restricting the ability
  to make such judgments of conscience—through such factors as
  poor parenting, faulty education, mediocre entertainment and
  irresponsible life styles.

- Third, it can be damaged by political restrictions on the ability to act freely and in line with those judgments of conscience.

It is disturbing how recent events show that these trends are underway, even in America, and that this "inherent, inalienable and inviolable right" is no longer considered important or understood, even by ostensible champions of human rights. In 1834, Daniel Webster could justifiably boast: "Wherever you go, you find the United States held up as an example by the advocates of freedom. The mariner no more looks to his compass or takes his departure by the sun, than does the lover of liberty think of taking his departure without reference to the Constitution of the United States."[17]

A cornucopia of quotations could be cited in the same direction, and soon after his election President Obama praised the U.S. Constitution in similar words: "The values and ideas in those documents are not simply words written into aging parchment, they are the bedrock of our liberty and security."[18] He even established January 16 as "Religious Freedom Day."

Later, in July 2012, Secretary of State Hillary Clinton published the U.S. International Religious Freedom Report for the year and delivered what was surely the strongest and most articulate defense of religious freedom by any U.S. government official ever. Religious freedom, she declared, was "the first freedom," the "essential freedom" and "what could be more fundamental to human dignity than that?" "The world is sliding backward," and "Governments have a solemn obligation to protect the rights of all citizens." As for the administration of which she was a part, "We will continue to advocate strongly for religious liberty."[19] Running for reelection in 2012, the president was equally emphatic. "My commitment to protecting religious liberty is and always will be unwavering."[20]

Such rhetoric was genuinely stirring, but somehow there was a huge contradiction. Was it just hypocrisy, the difference between the administration's words and actions? Was there a gap between America's foreign and domestic policy? Or were the president and his team unaware of the gap between their promises to religious believers and their actions on behalf of their special interests, and in particular the supporters of the sexual revolution? For earlier that very year, defenders of religious freedom were scrambling to get President Obama to take their rights seriously, as the White House delivered a massive three-punch blow to freedom of thought, conscience and religion as it had long been established in American history and experience.

- First, the administration mandated that religious organizations purchase health insurance that covered "cost-free" abortion drugs, sterilization and other contraceptive services that were clearly known to violate the strong, settled religious convictions of some religious believers.

- Second, they offered these organizations a period in which they could adjust their views to this requirement, as if conscience-based convictions could be tailored easily.

- Third, they later announced an "accommodation" whereby the insurance companies would pay for the services rather than the religious organizations themselves.

No one was fooled by the offered accommodation. The mandate was a violation of conscience by a direct command, and the backlash was as furious as it was predictable. What mattered was not the cost-free offers or who the final dispensers were, but the services themselves. Certain religious individuals and organizations, such as Roman Catholics, were being required to provide or to cover insurance for services that as a matter of deep conviction they deeply believed were immoral. If they passed on the act of dispensing to the insurance companies, the religious organizations would still be paying the companies and the companies in turn would pass back the cost to the religious organizations. In short, the government was proposing a shell game. One way or another the religious organizations would be paying for the services to which they objected as a matter of moral conscience.

No tumbrils rolled, no fires were lit, and no hangmen came to do their dread duty. But thank God that Madison's "first experiment upon our liberties" still created alarm as it did in 1785. Such a deliberate, flagrant violation of freedom of conscience by self-professed American liberals was stunning and outrageous, and many religious groups, including Evangelicals, Mormons, Muslims and Sikhs, at once stepped forward to stand with the Roman Catholics and take their place in the protest.

It is now time, Mr. President and all who succeed you in the Oval Office, to walk the talk. Ringing rhetoric on its own is only the rouging of the face of a wounded liberty. There is merit to your argument that those who take so much public money should expect to abide by government regulations—but not at the expense of freedom of conscience! You have set in motion violations of conscience that must be reversed if you are to protect freedom and be true to your own words and your own heritage.

Was the violation the intention of the president himself or the result of the pressure of the LGBT lobby (the coalition of lesbians, gays, bisexuals and transgenders)? Was it deliberate or inadvertent? My own guess in each case would be the latter, because of the president's own Christian faith, but it mattered little. In the one-word title of the united response, it was "Unacceptable." As the signers of this statement declared in response, "It is an insult to the intelligence of Catholics, Protestants, Eastern Orthodox Christians, Jews, Muslims, and other people of faith and conscience to imagine that they will accept an assault on their religious liberty if only it is covered up by a cheap accounting trick."[21]

So I Didn't Speak Up

Many significant points were drowned out in the ensuing hullabaloo, including the fact that the administration was undercutting its own ideal of universal health care. With more than five thousand hospitals in America, Catholics were pioneers and supporters of universal health long before political liberalism took up the cause, and will be long afterward too, whatever the restrictions on their freedom.

Unfortunately, too, the effect of this strong protest on behalf of freedom of religion and belief was blunted because many of those who took it up did so in a spirit that was purely political. With the Democratic Party becoming increasingly the secular party and the Republican Party largely religious, the issue of freedom of religion and belief is in great danger of becoming partisan rather than principled. Among conservatives, concern for the principle was lost in the general opposition to the president and their diehard wish to see him defeated at any cost, in any way and over any issue. For liberals who were still concerned for religious freedom, the violation was clear and egregious, but it was apparent that they found themselves politically uncomfortable and shrinking in numbers.

In short, freedom of religion and belief lost both ways: mainly from the mandate of the administration that made such protestations on behalf of this very freedom, but in part too from the politicized response of the opposition.

Earlier in Britain in 2007, the Sexual Orientation Regulations came into force, requiring all adoption agencies that wished to receive public funds to offer their services to homosexual couples. In a so-called compromise, Prime Minister Tony Blair offered such agencies two years to adapt to these new policies or close. Later when Roman Catholics cited freedom of conscience to explain their refusal go against their fundamental convictions over the issue, the chairman of Britain's Equality and Human Rights Commission pronounced that religious believers "aren't above the law."[22] In a modern echo of the dreaded Star Chamber of Williams's time, he declared that they must choose between their faith and obeying the law when their beliefs conflict with the will of the state.

Indeed they would and did.

Two years later, in 2009, the new U.K. Supreme Court waded into direct interference with theological matters when it ruled that an Orthodox Jewish school in London that had refused admission to a boy was guilty of racial discrimination. By traditional Jewish standards of matrilineal descent, the boy was not Jewish because his mother was Italian, but the millennia-old criterion of matrilineal descent was brushed aside in the name of avoiding racial discrimination. Freedom of thought, conscience, religion and belief was once again trampled on thoughtlessly in the name of equality, and with an irony typical of equality drives, the pursuit of nondiscrimination became the grounds for a new form of discrimination.[23]

Pastor Martin Niemöller's famous postwar confession and warning has been cited and adapted again and again by many who do not want to see a repeat of the terrible mistake of the 1930s: "They came first for the Catholics, but I wasn't a Catholic, so I didn't speak up . . ." With the dark reminders of their European past ever present, including the recent British decisions against them, not only Catholics but Jewish commentators were quick to read the warning signs in the actions of the Obama administration:

> Today it is contraception and the morning-after pill. Tomorrow it will be kosher slaughter, or matrilineal descent, or circumcision, or other matters of existential importance to Jewish observance. If the Obama administration gets away with forcing Catholic institutions to step across lines of life and death in the name of "health," the federal government

will have a precedent to legislate Judaism out of existence—
as several other countries have already tried to do.[24]

Some of the public responses to these incidents were disheart-
ening—"What was all the fuss about?" many people said, and as in
the 1930s, passed by on the other side of the street. It was plain
that ignorance about the history and importance of freedom of
conscience was widespread. As if "they came first for the religious
people, but I wasn't religious, so I didn't speak up."

A darker response was more disturbing. A student said to me in
a university discussion, "Religious people have it coming to them.
This is payback time for their record in the past." What he had in
mind, he explained, was the coming retribution that he believed
Christians and other religious believers deserved. It was time for
them to pay, not only for the more recent abuses of the Catholic
coverup of the pedophile crimes and the follies of the Christian
right, but for Christian opposition to gay and lesbian lifestyles and
for the whole record of Christian crimes down the centuries.

Such anger is irrational and surely fueled in part by anxiety. But
that student and others like him often seem completely unaware of
what they are doing to themselves. When societies are in decline, it
is common to turn against the old faith that made them what they
are. In that sense, the present moment in the West is characterized
by an ABC mood (Anything But Christianity). People will believe
any weird, wild and wonderful thing except the old faith. But such
an attitude and the vengeful spirit that goes with it easily spills
over into an illiberalism that hurts the liberal most of all.

FREEDOM BETWEEN THE EARS IS NOT ENOUGH

These open challenges to freedom of religion and belief are not the
end of the problem, for religious freedom in the West has been
caught in the toils of a thousand confusions and controversies. The

ringing proclamations of soul freedom by Roger Williams and others far outstrip the feeble statements about freedom of worship that we have heard from Western leaders more recently. After all, the oppressive governments of China, Iran and Saudi Arabia routinely acknowledge freedom of worship and are just as happy to routinely ignore it.

In light of the costly and hard-won history of freedom of thought, conscience, religion and belief, and America's pioneering role in it, such pathetic defenses are shameful, especially by American leaders who ought to know better. Either their statements were weak because the speakers were ignorant of their own history. Or worse, they watered down their statements deliberately to appease such powerful interests as Middle Eastern oil that they wish to mollify for other reasons. Either way, such statements are woeful and a disgrace to any who would consider themselves champions of humanity and human rights.

Far better the plain and simple declaration of America's First Lady, Michelle Obama, to an African Methodist Episcopal Church: "Our faith journey isn't just about showing up on Sunday. *It's about what we do Monday through Saturday as well.*"[25] And for that, freedom of worship will never be enough. Free exercise is what is required.

If *soul liberty* was Roger Williams's seventeenth-century term for freedom of thought, conscience, religion and belief, *free exercise* was James Madison's brilliant insertion into the final draft of the Virginia Declaration of Rights in May 1776. At one stroke it advanced freedom by light years by showing the full logic of soul freedom. Far more than simply freedom of worship, it's about what we do Monday through Saturday as well.

On the one hand, it replaced John Locke's older and weaker term *toleration*, which George Mason had originally drafted. Whereas toleration is always preferable to its opposite, intolerance, it is never more than a matter of condescension: the powerful tolerating the weak, the government tolerating the citizen and a majority tolerating a minority. In bold contrast, the *free exercise* of freedom of religion and belief is an inherent and inalienable right that no government has the right to give and no government has the right to take away.

On the other hand, free exercise goes beyond mere freedom of worship to include the rich, full freedoms mentioned earlier—the right to profess, practice and propagate faith too. Historically, all these components were included under the right to free exercise, and thus the freedom to practice one's faith throughout life and throughout society, in public as well as in private—subject of course to the limits of the equal rights of others and the limit of the rule of law.

It has always been the aim of tyrants to limit freedom to the tiniest space possible—the space between our two ears, with our mouths shut. In that sense, a believer in a prison cell is always free to worship in his or her heart. But it is always the glory of free societies to enlarge soul freedom to the maximum extent possible for people of all faiths and none. Freedom, then, should be measured by the standard of free exercise rather than freedom of worship, and this provides a gauge by which a free society can be measured. Liberals and conservatives together should reflect on this yardstick as a core element of the accordion-like character of religious freedom: *The wider the sphere of full freedom of religion and belief for all, in public and in private, the healthier is the state of freedom in a society. Conversely, the smaller the sphere of full freedom of religion and belief for all, the poorer is the state of freedom.*

By this standard, it is evident that England and the United States, the two original champions of early modern freedom, are facing attempts to make their societies far less free than they once were. The accordion is being squeezed shut, and while a closed accordion is still an accordion, it can make no music unless it is opened and draws in air. Those who seek to restrict free exercise to the private sphere alone are no friends of freedom in the tradition of Roger Williams, John Milton, James Madison and John Stuart Mill.

Today, Madison's magnificent term *free exercise*, which in 1791 was enshrined in America's Bill of Rights, is now increasingly entombed in the National Archives and fighting for its life amid the acrid attempts of secularists to ban it from public life. It still shines down in giant letters onto Pennsylvania Avenue from the walls of the Newseum in Washington, DC. Sadly, however, what adorns America's walls no longer animates the minds of many Americans. Saddest of all, the ignorance and neglect are most striking among Williams's English heirs, Madison's American heirs and in the liberal universities that were once the guardians of freedom of thought, conscience, religion and belief.

INTERLOCKING AND INSEPARABLE

Mention of the family of rights is a reminder that when the American founders called freedom of conscience the "first liberty," they were not out to create a hierarchy of rights. That would have been invidious. They were simply expressing their understanding of the logical relations between the different rights in the cluster of core political freedoms.

The truth is that no human right confers an unlimited freedom, no single human right is more important than another, and there will never be an absolutely correct answer or universal approval of many of the decisions affecting the application of human rights. Together, however, freedom of religion and belief and all other human rights are interlocking and inseparable, as a moment of thought would show.

The right to freedom of assembly or association assumes and requires the right to freedom of speech. In that sense, freedom of

speech logically comes before freedom of assembly. Free people
want to join together with other people not merely to talk about
the weather or some inconsequential subject—though that too
would be covered by the protection of the right—but because they
want to say things to each other that matter to them supremely.

In the same way, freedom of speech assumes and requires
freedom of conscience, and in that sense freedom of conscience
logically comes before freedom of speech. Free people want to
speak freely of things that matter to them supremely—matters of
truth, justice, freedom, human dignity, beauty, social policy and
the like—because they are convinced of them and are therefore
bound by the dictates of their conscience.

Thus freedom of religion and belief was logically the first
liberty—and it was also the first historically. As recently as the eminent Jewish lawyer Leo Pfeffer, it was firmly held that only *as*
freedom of conscience was fully guaranteed—and *so long as*
freedom of conscience was guaranteed—that the other freedoms
would remain secure.[26] Freedom of conscience was therefore the
pattern and pacesetter for the other liberties, and without it the
others—and liberty itself—would neither work nor last.

Importantly too, freedom of religion and belief is both a right
and a responsibility. It is often said that eternal vigilance is the
price of liberty, but liberty carries a daily bread-and-butter price
even before that—the primacy of duties before rights. Freedom
therefore stands in strong contrast to the dutiless modern notion of
freedom of choice, which is all rights and no responsibility, and
grows simply out of the sovereignty of the chooser as consumer.
For its pioneers freedom of thought and conscience was a right
that grows out of a responsibility and carries a responsibility.

- First, freedom of religion and belief carries a responsibility and
  a duty to what it is that we each believe, which is why when we

act on it, we are bound to it by the dictates of our conscience. We are subjects of truth rather than sovereigns over truth. Bound by the dictates of conscience, we have no choice. Like Martin Luther at the Diet of Worms, those bound by the dictates of conscience are to be respected because they can "do no other." In that sense, freedom of conscience for religious believers is always "under God," regardless of the legality of the term in public life.

- Second, freedom of religion and belief carries a responsibility because it entails a duty we owe to ourselves. All freedom requires order and therefore some restraint, yet the only restraint appropriate to freedom is self-restraint, which means that both free individuals and free peoples always require self-governance in order to become free and remain free.

- Third, freedom of religion and belief carries a responsibility because it is a duty we owe to all others, and all others owe to us, in that it is mutual, reciprocal and universal. As I have stressed constantly, a right for one is a right for another and a responsibility for both.

In sum, to override freedom of conscience through law, coercion, torture, bureaucratic regulations or any form of government or social pressure, including political correctness, is oppressive and unconscionable. On matters of conscience, free people must always be persuaded and never coerced.

NOTHING COMES CLOSE

In parts of the world today it is fashionable to discount freedom of thought and conscience as a Western notion and culturally relative to boot. Other notions have been put forward in its place as culturally equivalent. The Confucian notion of "two-man mindedness," for example, was a key notion in the development of the Universal

Declaration of Human Rights, just as the Arab notion of hospitality is much mentioned today. (Hospitality, Prince Ghazi of Jordan reminded Pope Benedict, is one of "the cardinal virtues of the Arabs . . . in some of the hottest and most inhospitable climates" in the world. "Arab hospitality means not only loving to give and help, but also being generous of spirit, and therefore appreciative."[27]) Other equivalents include the Jewish ethic of love for the stranger, Hippocrates's maxim "Do no harm," the Buddhist notion of compassion (paralleled in many faiths), the Koran's notion of competition in goodness, and of course the Golden Rule and the Silver Rule.

Some of these companion notions are both illuminating and helpful. But no one concerned to stand for soul freedom for people of all faiths should have any doubts. None of these other notions comes as close to highlighting and protecting what freedom of conscience guarantees—and for everyone without exception. After all, at its heart freedom of conscience stands for the safeguarding of the rights of human thought and expression that are *equal, universal, reciprocal and mutual rights for all the citizens of the world.*

To be sure, these rights originated in certain parts of the West, but they were established only after costly stands against oppressive and entrenched abuses of powers in the West. And today, like a boomerang, these universal rights come back to hit Western nations and Western presidents and prime ministers too, whenever and wherever they too are in violation of fundamental rights—as so often they are today.

Other important ideas and other ethical standards from around the world are welcome to join hands with soul freedom to protect human liberties and guarantee justice. But they must speak for all humankind, and they must not be a cover for promoting or privileging any one religion, such as the protection of Islam through notions such as defamation.

And there must be no misunderstanding: No other concept or ideal has so far rivaled freedom of thought and conscience and free exercise for their clarity, strength and proven historical success in promoting and protecting human freedom. To surrender them cravenly today in the name of a fashionable political correctness, a misguided ecumenism, a muddle-headed multiculturalism or a craven appeasement to powerful interests would be a monumental folly for the appeasers and for the interests of the world.

Freedom also requires that we be frank. There are leading Muslims around the world who are deeply committed to freedom of religion and belief for all, including the freedom to convert from Islam. Some indeed have stood for the principle at great cost, even at the cost of their lives. But there still needs to be a far wider acknowledgment of an elementary and undeniable fact: Religious persecution is far more common and far more severe in Muslim-majority countries than elsewhere in the world, and societies that are grounded in Sharia law have proved especially dangerous to freedom of religion and belief for all people.

A WELLSPRING OF CIVIL SOCIETY

The prime importance of freedom of thought, conscience, religion and belief should be sufficient by itself, but there are other supporting reasons why soul freedom is so crucial. The first is that soul freedom stands as an enduring wellspring of civil society. This is the positive consideration that counters the erroneous view that "religion poisons everything," as Hitchens loved to state so baldly. Arguably, there are many influential gifts to modern civilization that come directly or indirectly from religion—including philanthropy, reform movements, the university, the rise of modern science and human rights themselves. But regardless of the past, all who today appreciate the importance of Edmund Burke's "little platoons," Peter Berger's and Richard Neuhaus's "mediating structures," and Robert

Putnam's "social capital" can have no question that faiths and faith-based communities of many kinds have a unique and unrivaled role to play in nongovernmental initiatives around the world.

As the long history of Western charity, philanthropy and reform proves, almost all the great movements of Western reform have been inspired by faith and led by people of faith. This was true from the banning of infanticide to the stand against the Conquistadores by Bartolomé de las Casas, to the abolition of slavery by William Wilberforce, to the civil rights movement under Martin Luther King. To argue otherwise is not only ludicrous but silly and unworthy of any but the most blinkered thinkers. It is unquestionably true that religions have acted at times as a poison in human affairs, but it is no less true that faith has also shone as the guiding light for many of humankind's greatest advances in justice and freedom.

Richard Dawkins is correct that he is not responsible for the fact that his ancestors made their fortune as slave owners in eighteenth-century Jamaica and were diehard opponents of Wilberforce's movement to abolish slavery. But at the same time he is niggardly in his failure to acknowledge freely that faith played the unquestioned and decisive part in the liberation of the slaves and the abolition of the scourge of the slavery that his forebears supported so stubbornly. There is far more that faith has done for humanity than Dawkins's blinkered eyes have seen or his prejudiced mind has so far acknowledged.

To be sure, what Paul Hawken calls today's worldwide "movement of movements," which is fighting for justice, for the earth and for indigenous peoples, is made up of dedicated secularists as well as members of most of the world's faiths.[28] But the role of faith is undeniable. So also is the realization that a vital civil society requires an open civil public square if such faiths are to be free to make their contribution.

Many people view social entrepreneurialism as a trickle-down effect of the triumph of market capitalism and its keynote feature: entrepreneurialism. But in fact social entrepreneurialism is far older, for freedom of conscience and its corollary, free exercise, liberate faith in the same way. Thus, what demonopolization and a level playing field does to liberate business, freedom of thought and conscience as an equal right for all does to liberate faith communities. Under the conditions of freedom of thought and conscience for all, a level playing field is created for all faith communities. Each stands on its own feet. Each has a faith that is voluntary and not coerced. Each has its own rights and its own opportunities. No longer can any faith community look to "the sword" and "the purse" of the state to protect its interests and promote its cause. Each is therefore only as strong and active as its members' faith, vision, generosity and dedication.

Put differently, there are strong links between a civil society and a free market of ideas, and freedom of thought, conscience and religion is a basic requirement of both. Freedom of thought, conscience, religion and belief is therefore at the heart of any free market of ideas, and also vital to economic development, technological advance, democratic politics and artistic creativity.

Paradoxically, too, robust debates in the free competition of ideas promote not only creativity but stability, for when there is a robust clash of ideas, the truth claims of the irrational, the dangerous and the extremist can be shown up for what they are. Conversely, the sunlight of debate is a powerful solvent to ideas that are inherently weak as ideas or dangerous as policies, but which gain in strength the more they are repressed. As Oliver Wendell Holmes argued, "the best test of truth is the power of the thought to get itself accepted in the competition of the market."[29]

This impulse to enterprise at the heart of freedom of conscience is precisely what has periodically activated many of the most successful initiatives in progressive education, generous charity and courageous reforms throughout history—and as the work of many of the great religious NGOs (nongovernmental organizations) attests, it still does. It was precisely when faith communities were freed from all government dependency that they made their greatest contributions. They were truly voluntary and therefore doubly free—free negatively because free from government dependency, and free positively because free to undertake the entrepreneurial visions with which their faiths inspired them.

The burgeoning activism and social entrepreneurialism of faith communities in the global era is remarkable. There is no limit to their potential for tackling ills of all kinds and advancing freedom and justice. But let there be no mistake: there would equally be no flourishing of these movements without the freedom to dream, to volunteer, to give and to engage, all of which are guaranteed and guarded at the heart of freedom of thought and conscience and free exercise.

Block freedom of thought and conscience, as Britain did over the Roman Catholic Church and orphanages and the United States did over the health mandate, and you choke the vital wellspring of social entrepreneurialism. Penalize religious NGOs that cannot agree with the narrow LGBT agenda, as the Obama administration was threatening to do, and you will kill the goose that lays the golden egg.

Take note, presidents, prime ministers and principals at all levels of society, there is no question where the prime source of our Western culture of giving and caring comes from. But you cannot have the golden egg without the goose that lays it, and not even the most gigantic and beneficent inflation of Leviathan could ever compensate for the loss of a thriving civil society. Indeed, the state would bankrupt itself in the process of trying to do what the faith-based communities do so naturally and so much better.

THE KEY TO SOCIAL HARMONY

The other supporting reason why soul freedom is important is that it provides the key to social harmony, both within societies and between them. The latter is easily stated: Countries that take religious freedom seriously are not a threat to others, whereas countries that violate freedom of religion and belief are a serious threat. The external and the domestic are closely related. President Hu Jintao of China used to speak fervently and often of his dream of China's "harmonious society," but his solution for blending diversity and maintaining harmony was fraudulent because it was merely another name for coercion. In Indonesia in 2006, President Yudhoyono passed a decree on behalf of "religious harmony," but Muslim activists have used it to close more than four hundred churches.

The term *harmonious society* ducks the real issue facing China, Indonesia and the world today: True human flourishing requires a form of harmony that blends diversity with genuine liberty. Diversity without liberty is routine policy for authoritarian regimes, but humans are not slaves to governments or ideologies, whether Marxist in China, Muslim in Iran, or pansexual in the West. In the advanced modern conditions of the global era, the challenge of our time is to blend diversity with liberty and still create harmony.

No country in history has a perfect record over this task. Even if it did, it would not help us in our exploration because there is no such thing as a uniform one-size-fits-all solution to the problem of living with our deepest differences. The American, the French and the English settlements that I mentioned will always be different from the Chinese, the Russian and the Indian settlements—not to speak of the Egyptian, the Brazilian, the Indonesian, the Iranian, the Kenyan and all the other settlements of the world.

Each country has the right to its own heritage. In the light of its own unique history and its own cultural values, it has to work out its own solution and build its own settlement. In England, for example, the Church of England is so intertwined with English customs, traditions and institutions that any hasty disestablishment would be an act of culpable folly. But at the same time, different countries must each work out in their own different and unique settlement a deliberate and steady expansion of the spheres in which the three core human rights are advanced and protected. Within their own settlement, which may certainly be different from their neighbors and from the rest of the world, they must each work out the fundamental first principles that are the rights for all citizens and universal for all the countries of the world—freedom of thought and conscience, freedom of speech and freedom of assembly.

Different societies can therefore be gauged and judged by their success or failure in expanding these spheres of freedom. Mere declarations, stirring civic rhetoric and even strong legal constitutions will never be the real test of their success. *To the degree that a society has truly widened the spheres of freedom for all its citizens in practice, it can be judged to be truly free. But to the degree it refuses to do so, or no longer continues to do so, it does not deserve the name of freedom, regardless of its rhetoric and regardless of its previous record.*

Admirers of America are often saddened by its present failure to live up to the promise of its past and at such a moment. But many supporters of freedom of thought and conscience would gladly pay tribute to Madison's "true remedy" as the most nearly perfect settlement of religion and public life that the world has seen so far— the last fifty years excepted. For by guaranteeing full protection for freedom of thought and conscience for all, the American founders allowed for a system in which strong religious convictions and strong political civility complemented each other rather than contradicted each other.

There have certainly been egregious violations of religious liberty in American history, even after the great leap forward of the First Amendment—for example, the ugly Know-Nothing nativism of the discrimination against Roman Catholics, Jews and Mormons in the nineteenth century, actions against minority religions such as the

Branch Davidians more recently, and the widespread anti-Muslim bigotry now. But as I said, the founders may have erred badly in their treatment of race and women, but they corrected the errors of Puritan New England and Anglican Virginia and got freedom of religion and belief almost nearly right from the start. Americans tend to yawn at anything as obvious as the genius of the First Amendment, but a comparison with the rest of the world shows its distinctiveness.

Many parts of the world, such as postwar Western Europe before the arrival of the tidal wave of recent immigrants, and with the exception of Ulster, showed a remarkable civility toward religious differences (though there was, and is, a glaring blind spot toward minority religions, usually termed *cults*). But the overall civility of this period was no great achievement because, in an increasingly secular age, there was relatively little religion to be uncivil about. Elsewhere in the world, such as the Middle East, there was the opposite problem. There were such strong religious convictions that there was no civility, no liberty and often most tragically, no life—even within the same religion.

Better than most countries in history, the United States has maximized diversity, liberty and harmony together. In so doing, the best of American history demonstrates the critical importance of the presence of freedom of religion and belief, just as the last fifty years of culture warring equally demonstrates its absence.

Again, it is time, and past time, to ponder the question. What does it say of us and our times that the Universal Declaration of Human Rights could not be passed today? And what does it say of the future of freedom of thought, conscience, religion and belief if it can be neglected and threatened even in the United States, where it once developed most fully—that it can be endangered anywhere? Who will step forward now to champion the cause of freedom for the good of all and for the future of humanity?

5

DEATH BY
A THOUSAND CUTS

THE FOURTH STEP IN THE REVALUATION *is to recognize the thousand and one small ways by which freedom of thought, conscience, religion and belief is being eroded in the West, and to see how these seemingly trivial incidents add up to a rising constriction on freedom and therefore to a Western failure to assume much-needed leadership on the issue in the world.*

"If you're so concerned about religious freedom for everyone, why don't you go to China or Iran and try your arguments out there? And while you're at it, why don't you preach it to the Taliban too and see what happens? What's going on in the West is nothing compared with the crescendo of evils elsewhere in the world. What you're doing is straining at a gnat and swallowing a camel."

That spirited objection came up in a university discussion not so long ago, and of course the objector had a point. There is no question of moral equivalence. The damage done to freedom in the Western controversies and culture wars is a mere pinprick compared with the brutal evils of government repression and the savagery of sectarian violence in other parts of the world. But the objector missed the point that I was making. Western violations of freedom of thought, conscience and religion may be pinpricks compared with the sickening butchery elsewhere, but seen another way, they are momentous in significance.

- First, there is no way around the fact that such seemingly petty violations are still just that—violations of a primary, foundational and painfully won human right.

- Second, those who commit these violations show the vast carelessness of the complacent to the lessons and costs of the long, hard road toward freedom and justice.

- Third, both those who commit the violations and those who shrug them off as insignificant represent a serious dereliction of Western responsibility. We are at a time when anyone with any experience at all of establishing freedom and justice for the common good needs to draw on their heritage and its lessons to humbly point a way forward for the world.

In other words, these Western violations are indeed slight in comparison with the violations elsewhere in the world, but soon their accumulated effect will lead to death by a thousand cuts. We should therefore watch out for such violations, if only to keep us vigilant toward the first assaults on our liberties. For, sadly, the slow erosions of time and the curious ironies of unintended consequences are helping to undermine the strong foundations for rights that we once had in the West, and this is true even in America where once they were defended so passionately.

THE CLOSING OF THE UNIVERSITY MIND

The primacy of the right to freedom of thought, conscience, religion and belief is now threatened openly by erosions and assaults from various sides—even by liberals and even in our colleges and universities. The so-called *L word* is still a proud and positive term for me, but sad to say, we are seeing a rising illiberalism from certain liberals who represent one of the gravest threats to freedom of thought and conscience in the Western world. This threat is further magnified when such inside illiberalism converges with an aggressive Islamic assault on freedom of religion and belief from the outside.

Communism in its Chinese form is a serious menace to freedom of thought and conscience, but mainly for its own citizens. It is too remote to threaten much of the rest of the world directly. Islam in its radical form is another menace, more dangerous to freedom than communism because it not only directly attacks the West from the outside, but also seeks to influence it from within. The present illiberalism now stalking the Western world is far less draconian than communism and far less overt than Islamism, but it is equally dangerous to freedom of religion and belief. It operates from inside the West, and at times from the highest and most prestigious levels of leadership, and it does so in the name of freedom itself and out of the best of intentions.

Does it smack of anti-intellectualism to talk of illiberalism in the university world? I will forever be grateful for the privilege of being educated at England's oldest and one of the world's finest universities. So it is painful to observe that so many colleges and universities have fallen captive to habits of politically correct thinking that undermine the freedom of thought and conscience for which they should be standing.

Yet perhaps that is not so surprising. Great universities have always been vulnerable to the winds of power and fashion in their day. What Roger Williams said of Oxford and Cambridge in the seventeenth century applies to many Western colleges and universities today. "We count the Universities the Fountaines [of knowledge] . . . but have not those Fountaines ever sent what streams the Times have liked? And ever changed their taste and colour to the Prince's eye and Palate?"[1]

One example of flowing with "the streams the times have liked" and catering to the Prince of Opinion's eye is the spreading rash of American universities seeking to "derecognize" religious groups on campus that refuse to alter their fundamental beliefs to suit current regulations in the name of equality and nondiscrimination. It would be patently absurd to refuse recognition to Hillel Societies that refuse to accept Muslims in their leadership positions, or atheist societies not open to having Hindus as their officers, or gay and lesbian organizations that would never allow Christian fundamentalists to stand for election as their executives, or sororities that might have a problem with men leading them. No self-respecting organization could waive its criteria for choosing its own leaders and expect to remain healthy. Doing so would be a recipe for institutional suicide. Yet Vanderbilt University became one of the latest in a series of universities that have refused to recognize Christian groups that do not allow all comers to run for their leadership positions.

No one disputes that all the main Christian groups at Vanderbilt have always welcomed all comers to their meetings. That was never the issue. But the administration refused them recognition because they sought to remain Christian in that they required their leaders to be Christian rather than all comers, and to subscribe to their expressly Christian beliefs. But how else are such groups to exercise their freedom of conscience, to remain free to what they believe to be true, based on the dictates of their conscience, and thus to be themselves and continue as organizations?

One Christian group applied for recognition from Vanderbilt with this clause concerning leadership: "Criteria for officer selection will include level and quality of past involvement, personal commitment to Jesus Christ, commitment to the organization, and demonstrated leadership ability"—only for the university administration to delete "personal commitment to Jesus Christ." Yet that was the sole criterion that made the group Christian and not Jewish, atheist, Buddhist or Mormon in the first place. No nation, no government and no university has the right to be the arbiter of religious belief, and no self-respecting liberal university should even think of trying to be. Yet Vanderbilt was imposing its own values on religious beliefs.

To be sure, Vanderbilt is a private university and as such has the right to lay down its laws and requirements within its own jurisdiction. And if religious groups are unwilling to abide by such laws and regulations, they are free to opt out of seeking such recognition. But that said, the policy is an egregious violation of freedom of thought and conscience, cloaked in politically correct language, and the loser is the overall richness and diversity of social life at Vanderbilt.

The university position is also an Orwellian overreach in the name of equality: Once again, some animals on the farm have become more equal than others. American universities are already known for many other fictions, such as "College sports are not about money," but this fiction should not be added to them. Freedom of thought, conscience, religion and belief is too important to be smothered by administration double-talk. Justice Robert Jackson wrote in the midst of the war-fueled anxieties of 1943, "If there is any fixed star in our constitutional constellation it is that no official, high or petty, can prescribe what is orthodox in politics, nationalism, religion, or other matters of opinion or force citizens to confess by word or act their faith therein."[2]

To be sure, too, Vanderbilt is not forcing anyone to disbelieve what he or she believes, or to believe what they do not believe. But they are "derecognizing" them for refusing to deny what they believe in the selection of their leaders. There is also a monumental irony in this case. Vanderbilt is a private university and its freedom to take this position is a matter of its constitutional associative right as it seeks to protect its identity and public message. But that is precisely the right that Vanderbilt wishes to deny the religious groups with which it disagrees.

As with free speech, th   s worthy
and appropriate for Vanc   o be the
university or the religiou   a liberal
university, that decision l   g ....unty and not
with university or its officials, however enlightened they believe themselves to be.

To add irony to irony, it was not so long ago that Vanderbilt excluded blacks from its undergraduate programs. In other words, the university already has a record of excluding those of whom it disapproves. Racism has gone, only to be replaced by political correctness. Unquestionably the damage is less extreme, but the dynamics of the illiberalism are the same.

Shame on Vanderbilt University, on its administration that designed this violation and its trustees who did nothing to stop it, but what really matters is the wider trend that goes beyond one university. It is sobering to see how well-meaning liberals can somersault into petty authoritarians, one minute standing as champions of diversity and the next as enforcers of uniformity. The same people who would decry inquisitions, intellectual censorship, ideological purges and all forms of ethnic cleansing are now the ones who in the name of egalitarian uniformity are conducting purges and cleansings of their own, and demanding open violations of freedom of thought and conscience.

Vanderbilt was not alone in its violations of religious freedom. Dartmouth also voted against a Christian organization because its bylaws required its leaders to be Christians—which was considered too exclusive, even though the same insistence was not applied to Atheists, Humanists, Agnostics at Dartmouth, or to College Democrats or College Libertarians. Clearly it was the Christian groups that were singled out, and once again it was almost certainly due to attempts to impose the new sexual orthodoxy.

To its credit, Harvard College, America's oldest and most prestigious university, has resisted joining this cavalcade of dishonor. Princeton and Cornell are among those that have reversed their decisions after insisting on a similar embargo for a while, and eminent universities such as the University of Florida, the University of Minnesota and the University of Texas have wisely granted exemptions for religious groups. When the issue was being debated at the State University of New York, Buffalo, the Student-Wide Judiciary forthrightly made a point that seemed to escape the notice of their own administration and the puritans at Vanderbilt, "It's common sense, not discrimination, for a religious group to want its leaders to agree with its core beliefs."

Article 11 of the Global Charter of Conscience affirms that not only individuals but groups have the right to freedom of thought, conscience, religion and belief:

> The rights of freedom of thought, conscience, and religion apply not only to individuals, but to individuals in community with others, associating on the basis of faith. Each person treasures the rights that inhere as in their person as an individual. Equally, each person treasures membership in families, communities, religious groups, and other deep affiliations that are essential to culture. The rights of peoples in association are membership rights, and they are as meaningful and significant as the rights we enjoy as individuals.

> No community of faith has rights that are superior to any other community, but the rights of thought, conscience, and religion are rights both for individuals and individuals in community because belief is both an individual assent and an associative practice. As such, religious groups must be free to govern their internal affairs free from governmental or outside interference in questions of doctrine, ethics, selection of leaders, design of organizational polity, the admission and

dismissal of members, and the future direction of the organization or community.

It goes without saying that derecognition by university administrators in the United States is far less draconian than derecognition of religious communities elsewhere in the world. In Sri Lanka, for example, where the laws protecting religious freedom are strong but meaningless, derecognition of the churches has also commonly meant death for pastors, destruction of church buildings, and internal displacement for hundreds of harassed members of the churches. But once again, these university cases matter because the difference is not one of kind, but degree, and Madison's maxim rings out again to his fellow Americans: "It is wise to take alarm at the first experiment upon our liberties."

Britain as ever falls in between the extremes. In 2012, in a typical act of middling derecognition, the U.K. Charity Commission denied charitable status to the 16,000-member Plymouth Brethren movement—the first time in British history that the government has denied status to a religious group on the grounds that it did not advance the public benefit. And why? Because the Plymouth Brethren restricted their service of Holy Communion to their own members (which the far bigger and more influential Roman Catholic Church has always also done). Even the established faith of the land was put on notice, when the commission's head of legal services announced: "This decision makes it clear that there was no presumption that religion generally, or at any more specific level, is for the public benefit, even in the case of Christianity or the Church of England."[3]

No Religious Voices Here

Where religion is disdained, religious freedom is discounted. An even more blatant example of the mounting illiberalism is the diverse secularist and separationist campaigns attempting to drive religion and religious voices from the public square altogether. Sometimes these initiatives come from aggressive secularists, such as America's Michael Newdow and Britain's Richard Dawkins, sometimes from groups advancing strict separation of religion from public life, such as the American Civil Liberties Union, and sometimes from the rising disgust at the crude unwisdom of religious voices in public life. But the outcome is a drive toward a secularist state orthodoxy that would be a massive disaster for freedom and for a foundational human right, as well as a drastic shrinking of the spheres of freedom in supposedly open societies.

The very concern behind the drive is misconceived. From Voltaire to Adam Smith, to David Hume, James Madison and Thomas Jefferson, the greatest Enlightenment thinkers have long recognized that the surest protection against a repressive establishment of any one religion or ideology is a multiplicity of religions. Voltaire, for example, compared the repressions of the state monopoly in his native France with the plurality he saw in London. France, which boasted many meat sauces, had only one religion and suffered from too little freedom, whereas England had a lamentable scarcity of good meat sauces, but allowed many religions and enjoyed far more freedom.

Today's self-professed heirs of the Enlightenment have somehow missed Voltaire's point. There is no question that we now have a greater diversity of faiths than ever, and the dominant worldwide trend is toward dismantling monopoly establishments, so for secularists to argue that any expression of faith in public life today is a dangerous return to an establishment is utterly absurd. To paraphrase H. L. Mencken, today's fundamentalist secularist is someone haunted by the thought that someone somewhere may just be breathing up a prayer in public.

Needless to say, the secularist strict separationism is not only absurd and illiberal, it is also blatantly self-interested. For if the secularists succeed in their bid to exclude all religion from public life, the result would be a strictly sanitized public square that favors secularism as the new de facto establishment. Yes, it is proper to talk of a secular state, in the sense that the state guards the freedom of all faiths and is impartial between them at that level. But a state requires its own values, and a secularist state is wrong, for that would mean a secularist state orthodoxy smuggled in through the back door.

There are many oddities in the strict separationists' attempt to cleanse public life antiseptically of all religion. In England, elite calls for strict separation represent a de facto disestablishment of the Church of England before any legal disestablishment has been decided by either Parliament or the people—which is surely the only explanation of the Alice-in-Wonderland situation where a government department can ban the wearing of the cross in the workplace when the cross is the official symbol of the official church of the land. And in the United States, similar calls for strict separation represent a decisive abandonment of the American founders' settlement in favor of the more extreme and even more unsatisfactory French *laicité*—without any understanding of the former or critical analysis of the latter.

But more is at stake than these smaller points. The deepest issue is the maintenance of freedom and an open society, which all true liberals should prize and protect. A nation that aspires to be an open society is a nation that seeks to expand the spheres of individual freedom throughout the whole of society, both private and public. But therein lies the contradiction of the strict separationists: The same liberals who would counter the government tendency toward secrecy by opening public life to greater scrutiny are the very ones who seek to reinforce the popular tendency toward apathy by closing public life against greater involvement by religious actors and voices.

Advocates of sunlight when it comes to freedom of speech, these liberals favor darkness when it comes to freedom of religion. Champions of inclusiveness when they fight for minorities, they become diehards for exclusion when they fight against the settled positions of a majority with which they disagree. Liberals in their private lives, they act like authoritarians in public life. One minute they are libertarians, denouncing anyone else who would impose their values on anyone else, and the next they act as Aristotelians, intent on using the law to make society good (or at least equal and progressive like them). Inconsistent at best and hypocrites at worst, such liberals need to face up to their own illiberalism, for how else are we to understand attitudes and policies that are brazenly undemocratic and intolerant, and an all-round shrinking of the spheres of freedom in societies that pride themselves on being open and free?

In Europe, the growing limitations on religions in public life come from two sources rather than one, and different sources too. On the one hand, more secularist countries such as France and Belgium are stressing their centuries-old concept of laicité to prevent further incursions of religion into public life. On the other hand, both varieties of Orthodox countries, Russian and Greek, are citing their even older fight against the incursions of Islam into Europe in order to justify their constraints on recent Muslim immigrants and other dangerous "sects," "cults" and minority religions.

Either way, what suffers is soul freedom as the freedom and right of all.

FREE PEOPLE PERSUADE AND ARE OPEN TO PERSUASION

A third and subtler example of illiberalism arises from the convergence between Western liberals and the more repressive forms of Islam and Hinduism in their common aversion to conversion, proselytism and apostasy. I say convergence as I presume it is unwitting, though some critics have charged that it is a conspiracy and quite deliberate—a liberal alliance with non-Western traditionalists to defeat the Western traditionalists who stand in the way of their liberal agenda. But unintentional or not, the effect is the same, and once again the outcome is illiberal.

Muslims openly espouse a double standard in their attempts to banish proselytism and the apostasy of conversion. They assert the freedom to share their own faith, and they welcome all who convert to Islam, but woe betide anyone who forgets which way the traffic moves on their one-way Sharia street. Iran has executed Baha'is for apostasy and considers them "unprotected infidels." Morocco routinely accuses and then deports foreigners under the charge of proselytism, even though sharing one's faith is protected in the Universal Declaration of Human Rights and in international law. And anticonversion laws in some parts of India are equally a blatant contradiction of freedom of religion and belief, and of other more open features of Indian democracy.

To be sure, liberal opposition to proselytism and conversion works at a different level, but if the violation is less, so also is the excuse. At an immediate and practical level, liberals who oppose proselytism and conversion forget that they are flouting the right to change one's belief that is expressly protected by Article 18 of the Universal Declaration. But at a far deeper level, they are also contradicting their own liberal commitment to rational persuasion.

It is now commonly argued that proselytism is wrong and should be banned for three reasons. First, it is said to be judgmental, because the persuader is arguing that someone else needs to be persuaded and is therefore judging the other person's views to be wrong. Second, proselytism is said to be coercive, because someone is trying to change someone else's mind and argue them out of what they now believe. And third, it is said to be culturally insensitive, because it threatens the integrity and autonomy of a community's right to be left alone to its traditions—"Conversions destroy community" and so on.

Such logic is highly selective, and we must always ask Lenin's question, "Who? Whom?" Clearly, for instance, the principle did not come into play with the Vanderbilt decision, and nor should it have as it is illiberal. It is also shallow and irrational, and would end in undermining all rational persuasion. After all, to be human is to search for truth, and we all have both a need and a right to be able to change our minds and our beliefs under certain circumstances.

Freedom to change our minds and our beliefs is implied in both the possibility of human error and the desirability of human growth. Contrary to much postmodern thinking and the fuzzy extremes of ecumenical dialogue, there are false and even dangerous beliefs, and there are views that are wrong and need rebutting. There is no better reason to change our minds than realizing that we were wrong about something or that we need to grow in understanding beyond the level we had reached before. At such moments the proper response to anyone who helps us see something we were ignorant of before should be gratitude, not resentment. There is in fact no argument against a person sharing his or her beliefs noncoercively that is not also an argument against rational persuasion, and no true liberal should have a quarrel with that.

Which of us has never been annoyed by someone buttonholing us on behalf of some cause or belief that we disagree with? Who has not been irritated by some tiresome attempt to convert us to a faith that we find repellent or ridiculous? But that does not justify the misguided movement to banish proselytism and conversion, whether outright through law or subtly through the unspoken pressures of political correctness. One person's persuasion has always been another person's proselytism.

On the Voltaire principle alone, we should all stand for the rights of those with whom we disagree who wish to persuade us—

liberals should fight for the rights of fundamentalists, Christians for the rights of Jehovah's Witnesses and Scientologists, and Muslims for the rights of atheists. All lovers of freedom should stand together against every insidious attempt to use the law to outlaw whatever is considered blasphemy, defamation or apostasy. It is time to rise up and challenge the politically correct. Who are the free thinkers now? Truly free people know what it means to persuade and to be open to persuasion.

UNDER THE HATCHES, UP AT THE HELM

A fourth and even worse example of illiberalism is more contentious. Certain homosexual and lesbian activists are advancing their own cause and attacking the freedom of religion and belief of those who disagree with them in a manner that undermines not only religious liberty but civil liberty too—and in fact all human rights.

This point needs stating with care, for it is certainly not true of all gay activists. It is unquestionable that many homosexual advocates clearly recognize that all human rights are for all citizens, and therefore advocate their claims with civility, honesty and an admirable fair-mindedness. From considerable personal experience, I have no doubt about that fact. But the claims of the vocal minority are not so careful and they require more attention than they have been given.

What I am saying may offend the current canons of political correctness, and some will automatically attack it as homophobia. But like any intolerant orthodoxy, political correctness has become a menace to genuinely liberal free speech. When serious issues are raised, they require a serious hearing. What is at stake here is crucial to the current crisis of freedom, and it must not be censored by any fascist-style silencing of the argument itself.

The Romans were unquestionably relaxed over the practice of same-sex relations. Julius Caesar, for example, was well known for his broad tastes in both men and women. Greek cities such as Sparta were even more so. But for two thousand years, Western civilization has followed the third of its three Mediterranean sources and built its core relationships on the heterosexual understanding of the family that was championed by the Jews rather than the Greeks and the Romans. As this long, stable and influential tradition is overthrown in a rapid, fifty-year social revolution, *relaxed* is hardly the word to describe either wing fighting the issue today. The plain fact is that many liberal activists are as zealous and intolerant as their opponents or the earlier Puritans are ever accused of being, so that in the explosively charged atmosphere of the culture wars, plain truths are left unsaid and unsayable.

Many gays and feminists have little sense of history, irony or self-criticism, or surely they would avoid the common pitfall of many of history's persecuted who became persecutors in their turn. Roger Williams and the early champions of religious liberty pointed out how those who had been oppressed easily became oppressors. Williams himself had crossed the Atlantic five times, and he repeatedly used the analogy of the ship of state to speak of civic affairs. His whole letter to the town of Providence in 1654 turned on that picture, but he used it earlier when he was incensed by the hypocrisy he saw in his fellow Puritans. Citing the strictures in Deuteronomy on those who cheat by using different weights in the marketplace, he excoriated the hypocrisy of those who spoke one way when they were "under the hatches," but treated others differently when they were "at the helm." This was precisely how "the new presbyter" became "the old priest writ large."[4]

In a similar way, some of today's gay and lesbian activists have morphed from being victims to being victimizers in politically correct uniform, for they routinely silence debate by turning any disagreement into the high-octane charge of bigotry, hatred, homophobia and holy terrorism. In the worst cases, when the charge is blind, untrue and unfair, the effect is to manipulate their opponents emotionally in a shameless power play of one-upmanship. I have seen the tactic used too many times. Such activists use their accusations to strike below the belt, aiming to surface the emotions of those who disagree with them. Which of us, after all, likes to be suddenly accused of hatred and bigotry? Those they assault then have to respond in one of two ways. Either they can react in kind with an emotional response and thereby appear to confirm the accusation leveled against them. Or they can smile bravely but weakly in order to contradict the charge, but then they have to stifle their real convictions and their true emotions, and find themselves on the back foot from then on in any discussion of the issue.

Even without this emotional bullying, those who wield the charge of homophobia routinely devastate the time-honored fundamental right of freedom of conscience and force people who disagree with them to kowtow to their newfound power regardless of freedom of thought and conscience. Sad to say, there is no question that homosexuals have faced real prejudice and hatred in the past, and sometimes continue to do so today, but to turn all honest disagreements into charges of hatred is a tactic that is dishonest, illiberal and in the end will backfire on them and their cause.

Only a Power Game

Yet that is not the worst of the tactics used by these extremists, and the deeper danger needs to be debated more than it has been. Their approach is to cite the precedent of the civil rights movement and so to use civil liberty, and in particular the principle of equality, to trump all considerations of freedom of religion and belief and promote their own agenda as a matter of civil rights.

The fact is that for any thoughtful exponent of human rights, a human right should never be outweighed by a civil right, for the former is inherent in humanity and the latter inherent only in a society that recognizes and grants it. This means that all human rights are automatically civil rights, but not all civil rights are human rights—they are the rights only in the societies that decide to recognize them. We are humans before we are citizens, and we are humans even when our citizenship is denied. Madison's insistence on this in his "Memorial and Remonstrance" is a striking part of his famous argument: "Before any man can be considered as a member of Civil Society, he must be considered as a subject of the Governor of the Universe. . . . We maintain therefore that in matters of Religion, no man's right is abridged by the institution of Civil Society, and that Religion is wholly exempt from its cognizance."[5]

Such distinctions are mere niceties to many of today's homosexual and lesbian activists. They show no concern at all when they not only abridge but annul the long-established and "inalienable and inviolable right" of freedom of thought and conscience in the name of their newly claimed civil right. The establishment of freedom of thought and conscience as the first liberty is one of America's historic achievements, yet these activists now describe the tension between religious liberty and civil liberty as a nonnegotiable zero-sum game—a game in which one must prevail and only one can be allowed to survive. When freedom of religion and belief and civil liberty clash, freedom of religion and belief is an obstruction.

In his survey of human rights, Britain's Equality and Human Rights Commissioner Trevor Phillips stated openly that in any clash with other rights such as transgender sexual rights, freedom of religion and belief is the expendable one that can and should be sacrificed. An employer "may legitimately refuse to accommodate an individual's religious beliefs where such accommodation would involve discrimination on the basis of other protected characteristics."[6] In other words, as with a floating exchange rate in economics, freedom of religion and belief is no longer an absolute right, and there is no gold standard by which it may be assessed. It is respected only as highly and as long as religion itself is respected, and we all know how high and long that would be in elite circles today. Religion is disdained, and so also can be religious freedom.

Do these zealots realize what they are doing? Only a fool saws off the branch on which he is sitting, yet these activists and equality commissioners are undercutting not only their opponents' rights but their own too, and in fact *all human rights altogether.* For when right is pitted against right, and a favored right is backed to win at the expense of a less favored right, the result is a Nietzschean moment that exposes the hollowness of all rights and shows that rights are really a matter of raw power.

What these activists are saying in effect is that religious freedom was once highly regarded because religion itself was influential— say, in Roger Williams's time in the seventeenth century, though even then the triumph of religious freedom came only after a costly victory over repression. It could then be said to be an inalienable right. But now, when religion and religious believers are viewed as marginal and retrograde in relation to the new inalienable right of the day, religious freedom is said to be an obstruction.

The dark logic of this dismissal of religious liberty in favor of civil liberty in a zero-sum game is blunt: *No rights are any longer inalienable and inviolable.* Liberalism itself then dissolves into a mere power player in postmodern power games, inalienability evaporates as a fiction, all rights talk is unmasked as a power struggle between interest groups, and both the Declaration of Independence and the Universal Declaration of Human Rights are rendered null and void. Indeed, the whole experiment in human freedom is exposed before the wider world as a monumental fraud.

As I mentioned earlier, Thomas Jefferson's famous question is carved like a trumpet blast on his memorial, "Can the liberties of a nation be secure when we have removed a conviction that these liberties are the gift of God?"[7] But his liberal heirs have turned his once-rhetorical question into a real one. If, as philosopher A. C. Grayling asserts, human rights are merely paper promises, an arbitrary convention created only by human decisions, then they are no more valuable and secure than the paper they are written on.

What one group or one generation decides, another can decide against, and that, for the *fiat* school of human rights, is the end of the matter. Power can speak one way at one time and another way at another time. Power can speak out of both sides of its mouth, and there is no principle above power to appeal to.

That is the point at which the role of judges and judicial activism may enter and play a pernicious part, acting against the rights of the democratic majority and even against the constitution of a country, such as the U.S. Constitution. In the normal course of things, judges with their power of judicial review stand as the supreme arbiter of the Constitution and its defenders of last resort. As such, they are rarely dangerous because they have too small a sphere of influence to be able to become despots in their own interests. But when judges are able to act on behalf of others in crucial situations, their power can be magnified enormously and decisive terms such as *constitutional* and *unconstitutional* can suddenly grow elastic and be used however the judges wish. As John Stuart Mill remarked, "A judge is one of the most deadly instruments in the hands of a tyranny of which others are at the head."[8]

THE PARADOX STRIKES AGAIN

The power wielders in such cases may be limousine liberals rather than Tidewater plantation owners, but the rights rhetoric is rendered as hollow as the rhetoric of the Declaration of Independence was said to be by postmodernists. All that matters for these zero-sum warriors and scorched-earth activists is power and their desire to win at all costs. As in the French revolution, when equality and conformity are prized above liberty and conscience, the result may be oppressive and ironic. For as Alexis de Tocqueville pointed out, "they had sought to be free in order to make themselves equal; but in proportion as equality was more established by the aid of freedom, freedom itself was thereby rendered more difficult of attainment."[9]

What these activists are demonstrating all over again is the enduring paradox of freedom—the greatest enemy of freedom is freedom—but this time with a liberal twist. In this case, it is liberals who are destroying human rights in the name of liberalism. Not only are they taking liberties with all our liberties, they are doing so in a way that destroys the basis of liberalism itself.

Earlier, I mentioned the angry contribution of a graduate student in a university discussion. "I'm a scientific atheist and a gay activist," he said with passion. "This is payback time. Religious people have it coming to them. We are going to use the power of the state to make sure we are never imposed on again." Gay activist? Scientific atheist? The first two identifications were legitimate, though like all positions open to debate, but a liberal authoritarian out to use the authority of the state to impose his will? The young man was too intense to pause long enough to reflect on the logic of his own candor, but his admission was revealing. Who is now imposing on whom? Who are the coercive ones in such cases? Lenin's power question, "Who? Whom?" is alive and well, and all human rights are the victims of such angry logic—their own liberal rights included.

All who love freedom and human rights must watch with care how certain activists, aided and abetted by certain government departments and certain judges, are coldly and determinedly disemboweling freedom of thought, conscience and religion as a fundamental principle, let alone as the first freedom. No fish caught in any river or ocean was ever gutted with such clinical efficiency as these activists are intent on gutting freedom of thought and conscience now.

Truly liberal societies are those that can accommodate differences and disagreements without resorting to coercion through law. Today's brave new radicals might as well cut out and publicly burn Article 18 of the Universal Declaration of Human Rights, but that would be too obvious. Article 18 can be destroyed by other, subtler means. Several Western societies face a crucial dilemma: What will be the status of freedom of thought, conscience, religion and belief if conscience clauses are routinely denied in the name of civil liberties thoughtlessly applied?

AT THEIR OWN RISK

"We must obey God, not human beings," cried the early Christian apostles, who refused to be coerced against their conscience—thus unleashing a principle that in the end would spell the death of Rome, its empire and its imperial authority.

"Here I stand. I can do no other," Martin Luther declared on the basis of conscience at the Diet of Worms—thus making the Reformation inevitable and unleashing the forces that brought down the repressive authoritarianism of the papacy and shaped the rise of the modern world.

"*Magna Carta* is such a fellow as he will have no sovereign," Sir Edward Coke cried as he resisted James I's principle of the divine right of kings and risked his own neck in the Tower of London—thus establishing the rule of law over the power of the monarchy, accelerating England's civil war, as well as the impetus behind the founding of the American colonies.

Through such stands as these, respect-for-conscience clauses have become an honored part of Western freedom, and those who think nothing of violating freedom of thought, conscience, religion and belief should remember such precedents and pause. This freedom cannot be abused with impunity, and the state or political party that attempts to do so will either succeed and harden into an unwelcome brutality of its own, or fail because it launches a movement against itself that will end by calling into question its very existence.

INCH BY INCH

In addition to these specific assaults, freedom of thought, conscience, religion and belief has also been eroded in more careless ways—an erosion that inch by inch may soon create a landslide. Religious freedom, some say, is simply "freedom for the religious." In one swipe, its universality is gone. It is merely a social luxury rather than a duty born of justice.

Again and again, America as the "land of the free" appears to be laying waste to its heritage as history's greatest champion of freedom of conscience. In a sad parody of the civil rights movement, freedom of conscience has been sent to sit at the back of the bus, while freedom of speech and freedom of assembly are ushered to the front. Increasingly, and even in the Supreme Court, religious freedom is defended in terms of freedom of speech rather than in its own right. And some even argue that the religious liberty clauses of the U.S. Constitution are like the appendix in the human body: superfluous and easily removed without consequence.

Again and again, America now gives the impression that its freedoms are in countless, small retreats—surrendering here in the name of national security, there in the name of health regulations, elsewhere in the name of protective safety, and often in the name of the new technologies and their ever-encroaching advance.

"Conscience and consciousness are the sacred precincts of the mind and soul," Rodney Smolla argues as a stalwart champion of free speech.[10] But he then goes on to wonder if *sacred* simply means "inaccessible," and what this might mean in the future. What if one day, through new technologies as yet not invented, the state is able to monitor not only our letters, phone calls and e-mails, but even our thoughts? In other words, when freedom of thought, conscience, religion and belief has been rendered void because the state can read our minds and patrol even our innermost thinking. Smolla's own answer is to seek to strengthen the case for human dignity, so he reinforces the famous maxim of Descartes: "I think, therefore I am *somebody deserving of respect.*"[11] But again, the question arises, why do we think we are worthy of such respect? Today there are too many answers to that question that would not pass muster, and too many people who have no interest in the question.

There was a time when the Western world knew differently, when freedoms were threatened more crudely and defenders of freedom were clearer and bolder in response. The recent slippages, shifts and erosions are all small, all gradual and anything but shocking and arresting like the horrendous violations elsewhere. But they need to be watched and assessed with equal care if we are not to throw away the freedoms that are our birthright with a carelessness that future generations will regard as irresponsibility, if not insanity.

Again, it is time, and past time, to ponder the question. What does it say of us and our times that the Universal Declaration of Human Rights could not be passed today? And what does it say of the future of freedom of thought, conscience, religion and belief if it can be neglected and threatened even in the United States, where it once developed most fully—that it can be endangered anywhere? Who will step forward now to champion the cause of freedom for the good of all and for the future of humanity?

6

DUELING VISIONS

THE FIFTH STEP IN THE REVALUATION is to analyze and assess the two major models on offer today, and to face the uncomfortable fact that, over the issue of living with our deepest differences, there are not only two competing visions but two extremes of the visions.

No one can follow the culture wars now embroiling the public life of many Western countries without seeing the fault lines between two grand visions of how religion and public life should be related. It is these visions that are in bitter dispute with each other. At first sight, the myriad changing issues at stake appear to be confusingly different—prayers in public spaces and on official occasions, head scarves or turbans in places of work, crosses or crescents worn as symbols of faith, the Ten Commandments as historical memorials or a religious expression, exemptions for conscience over practices such as adoption, abortion, contraception.

And so it goes. For fifty years in some countries, controversies such as these have made the public squares of the West into a cultural war zone rather than a forum for public deliberation and decision.

Yet closer inspection shows that all the kaleidoscopically changing controversies are an expression of the battle between two starkly different visions of public life—on one side, there are the proponents of what Richard John Neuhaus called a *naked public square*, those who would exclude religions and religious expression from public life; and on the other, the proponents of a *sacred public square*, those who would give some religion or ideology a preferred, established or monopolistic position in public life at the expense of everyone else. In short, the key difference is how we are to enter and engage public life when it comes to our religious and ideological differences.

DIFFERENT ROUTES, SAME END

To be sure, it is important to see that there are mild and strong versions of each model of the public square, and there are many societies that range somewhere in between. Take the different varieties of the naked public square, where all religion is excluded. The exclusion of religion sought by many American secularists and separationists is a relatively mild case, though it leads decisively in the direction of French-style *laïcité* rather the settlement constructed by their own founders. At the other extreme, the People's Republic of China practices a brutally harsh version of the naked public square that is the scourge of its people today and will be the shame of Chinese generations to come. The Beijing government is unashamed to flout human rights, persecute religious believers of many kinds, and without any qualms ruthlessly repress all signs of opposition to its totalitarian rule. In between these two extremes stands Kemal Atatürk's settlement for Turkey, which owes much to the French model, while seeking to accommodate a growing Muslim assertiveness, as under Prime Minister Recep Tayyip Erdoğan today.

A similar range can be seen among the varieties of the sacred public square. The Church of England stands at the mild end of the spectrum. It can truly say that it has no blood on its hands since the Glorious Revolution of 1688, and has therefore provoked no militant, French-style anticlerical hostility against itself. But today, its own government bans the wearing of the church's central symbol at places of work, and many of its friends fear that in its present institutional form the Anglican Church will not last another generation as England's established church. Little wonder that many of its adherents are described as "believing rather than belonging," and cynics say that the established church's amiable but feeble condition is fit only for the "hatching, matching and dispatching" of citizens (baptizing, marrying and burying), and should soon be disestablished as the Lutheran state church was in Sweden in 2000.

At the other end of the spectrum, harsh examples of countries with a sacred public square would include Iran, Saudi Arabia, Afghanistan under the Taliban and Burma under the generals. Their treatment of religions other than the established religion—Islam in the first three cases and Buddhism in the latter—is draconian, barbarous, a complete affront to human dignity and a monumental disgrace to the faiths they claim to espouse. Their blatant denials of freedom can no more be countenanced by the world than the brutally similar repressions by the Chinese and North Koreans.

What is clear is that, for all the variations on either side, neither of the two models fulfills the requirements of freedom and justice for all under the conditions of the exploding diversity of the global era. In truth, both models are now exposed as finally unjust and unworkable, and those concerned for humanity would challenge both of them on behalf of the primacy of soul freedom for each of the diverse faiths within their jurisdictions.

The conclusion is incontrovertible: Extreme versions of either model, China and North Korea on one side and Iran and Saudi Arabia on the other, are the world's major source of brutal governmental repression and the leading roadblock to advancing freedom and justice in the global era. Let there be no mincing of words when it comes to such roughshod flouting of human dignity. No secularist, however ardent, should defend the former, and no religious believer, however devoted, should justify the latter. The blood and tears of humanity cry out that there must be a better way.

TWEEDLEDUMS AND TWEEDLEDEES

A closer look reveals a further, though more controversial, fact. There is more extremism in the Western culture warring than many acknowledge, and this extremism is on both sides. Extremism rarely grows by itself. It grows in reaction to something. Extremism over religious issues is no exception, though because of people's philosophical prejudices and social locations, each side tends to see only one extreme: the other side. Everyone sees the extremism of the other side, but few admit the problem on their own side. The splinter in the other's eye looms large and dangerous, while the beam in one's own goes undetected.

In most educated circles in the West the extremism on the religious side sits in the stocks in the full glare of the media for all to deride and pelt. Indeed, for some people religion and extremism are synonyms. Unquestionably, few tyrants in history have matched the oppressive alliances between religion and government that end in coercing conscience and compelling belief. But little real thought seems to be needed to cook up some strong prejudices that run far beyond such facts.

Start with the single ingredient of a monopolistic religion. Throw in a mention of how established religions have dealt with dissenting opinion, such as the Inquisition, the slaughter of the Albigensians and the St. Bartholomew's Day massacre. Then season with a sprinkling of the contemporary cruelties of the Taliban or one of the idiotic acts of some purported religious leader, such as

Pastor Terry Jones's burning of the Qur'an. Stir according to taste, and the argument can be left to marinate to perfection. Plainly, religion is evil, divisive and violent—in fact, doubly evil for being evil in itself and evil too for the evils it rationalizes. Religion poisons everything.

Prepared according to such a recipe, the American religious right can clearly be served up as Al Qaeda with smoother chins, suaver manners and slicker PR. How else could otherwise fair-minded liberals pretend with a straight face that the Moral Majority, the Christian Coalition and Focus on the Family are "American ayatollahs," "American theocrats" and "American fascists"? Was it the American groups themselves they did not really investigate or was it the bogeymen they were comparing them to? Does it matter? According to the new atheists, religious moderates are no better than religious extremists. All are equally dangerous, and none are to be tolerated. Religious extremists are not to be tolerated, say Richard Dawkins and Sam Harris, but nor, they say openly, are religious moderates who tolerate extremists. By definition, religion itself is extremism.

This prejudice is not new. The philosopher Jeremy Bentham used to refer to organized religion as "Jug," which was short for juggernaut, as he charged that all religion was oppressive and rode over people like the infamous Hindu vehicle that crushed the devotees under its wheels. But in truth, he was blind to all that people of faith were doing even in his own lifetime. William Wilberforce, for example, was the greatest social reformer of all time and Bentham's contemporary, and never before had so many inspiring faith-based reforms been underway at the same time.

Fortunately, the crudely overt form of repression in the name of government-backed religion is rarer in today's world, though for that reason it stands out as uglier than ever. And, thank God, it creates a backlash against itself—for example, the worldwide revulsion at the barbarity of judicial punishments under the Taliban or at the indignity of the treatment of women under the Saudis.

Christian Reconstructionists in America are sometimes paraded as examples of dangerous Christian extremism, but they are a tiny group with no chance of wider political success, and only a paranoid should inflate their significance. Far more significant are the Islamist groups in the West that find themselves in Muslim-minority situations but still hew to the traditional Muslim-majority maxim that "Islam rules. It is never ruled." The result is a response summed up by Omar Ahmad, the cofounder of the influential Council on American-Islamic Relations (CAIR): "Islam isn't in America to be equal to any other faith, but to become dominant. . . . The Koran, the Muslim book of scripture, should be the highest authority in America, and Islam the only accepted religion on Earth."[1]

Such voices need to be repudiated emphatically, and first by other American Muslims. Sadly, they are not alone. Johari Abdul-Malik, director of outreach at the Islamic Center in Falls Church, Virginia, stated the goal of the Islamist *dawa* (mission) with equal candor: "Before Allah closes our eyes for the last time, you will see Islam move from being the second largest religion in America—that's where we are now—to being the first religion in America."[2]

Such a radical ambition of replacing the Constitution with a caliphate, combined with such a potentially dangerous political theology and backed by such a sizeable and growing community not yet integrated into Western ways, must be watched with hawk-eyed vigilance and countered with an unashamed allegiance to freedom of thought, conscience, religion and belief for all—including Muslims.

But who dares speak of the extremism on the secularist side? The present call for a partnership between responsible religious believers and responsible secularists is not a stalking horse for an assault on secularism, but the unashamed intolerance of the new atheists shows how there are secularist Tweedledees as well as religious Tweedledums. China's cultural revolution was an atheist inquisition for millions rather than thousands. The Hall of Infamy in the modern world includes Lenin, Stalin and Mao alongside Torquemada from an earlier time. If there is little religious freedom in Saudi Arabia, there is no more in China.

"Religion poisons everything," Hitchens cried, yet "Religion is poison" was the slogan Mao used to launch his vicious assault on the people of Tibet. If Al-Qaeda places bombs in the public square to kill, the ACLU puts up barriers in the public square to keep out, and the square is empty either way. For every Christian fundamentalist such as Jerry Falwell, there is a secularist fundamentalist such as Richard Dawkins. If there is the dire menace from theocrats, there is an equally dire menace from "seculocrats," those illiberal liberals who directly oppose all religion and seek to exclude all religious voices from public life.

When philosopher Bertrand Russell was the "Ditchkins" of his day (Terry Eagleton's combination of Dawkins and Hitchens), he was well known for his highhanded dismissals of religion in the name of rationalistic atheism. Yet Ludwig Wittgenstein, an even greater philosopher, once complained to a friend, "Russell and the parsons between them have done infinite harm, infinite harm."[3] The great atheist was as bad as the clerics he spent so much time attacking.

A century earlier Leibnitz had predicted, "The last sect in Christendom and in general in the world will be atheism." Its very way of propagating itself would show that "the world is already in its old age."[4] And a century after Wittgenstein, Eagleton comments similarly on Richard Dawkins, "His anti-religious zeal makes the Grand Inquisitor look like a soggy liberal."[5] Lord Patten, chairman of the BBC and chancellor of Oxford University, noted dryly, "It is curious that atheists have proved to be so intolerant of those who have a faith."[6]

Again, I am not claiming moral equivalence between the two extremes. Sometimes one side is the clear leader in infamy, sometimes the other. What matters is that neither extreme holds the answer. On one side, we face the very real problems of a sacred public square, with its advocates seeking to favor one religion at the expense of everyone else. On the other, we face the equally real problems of a naked public square, with its advocates seeking to force all religions out of public life and thus, at least unwittingly, to favor some form of secularism, whether atheism in the West or communism in China.

Dare anyone stand between the two sides when they fight in the same society? Who will step forward and declare, "A pox on both your houses"? The time has come for an honest recognition that each side can be as bad as the other, and that neither is the best model for the future. The need is for the courage to challenge both, not just the one that one side or the other happens to dislike more.

REACHING ACROSS THE DIVIDE

Allow me to address responsible religious and secularist leaders together, who realize that it is time to reach across the divide:

Religious leaders of the world, you for your part should face up to the modern world's inescapable challenge to the traditional standing of established or monopoly religions. We live at a time when fewer and fewer countries are dominated by a single religion or worldview, and all the beliefs of the world are either present or available everywhere. In the cumbersome jargon of the academy mentioned earlier, religions in the global era are increasingly becoming demonopolized, deconfessionalized and deterritorialized. It is no longer possible to defend the faiths in the old ways.

The result is that among the major challenges to you as traditional religious believers are:

- a frank acknowledgment of the past excesses and evils of religions
- an open recognition of the rights of all other religious believers
- an equal regard for the rights of the increasing number of citizens who are secularist in their ultimate beliefs

You who are secularist leaders across the world face no less a challenge. The same rights of freedom of conscience, the same realities of contemporary diversity and the same responsibilities of a civil public square all pose an equally fundamental challenge to you as secularists and to the notion of strictly secular public life in which religion is excluded from all public discussion and engagement. The worldwide resurgence of religions means simply that the global world has also been desecularized.

Thus, among the major challenges that face secularists are the following acknowledgments:

- a frank admission of the role of secularism in many of the world's recent oppressions and massacres
- an appreciation of the fact that the process of secularization is not necessarily inevitable or progressive
- a proper recognition of the rights of religious citizens in public life—the denial of which is illiberal, unjust and a severe impoverishment of civil society

Above all, it is time, and past time, for atheists to remove the fig leaf of the claim that they are simply nonbelievers and different from all the religious believers around them. A-theism merely says what atheists do not believe, but of course they too believe something. And for public discussion, that something is what matters. Call whatever atheists say they believe "secularism," call it "naturalism," call it "materialism" or trace it back through its genealogy and call it "Epicureanism" or "atomism," but be honest about the fact that it too is a worldview, an ultimate belief and a philosophy of life.[7] As such it deserves the same full freedoms of thought and conscience as any other worldview and philosophy of life—no less and no more. For too long a great deal of public discussion has been crippled by the myth that all religions are equal but those that are nonreligious are more equal than others.

Besides, a further lesson of the present polarizations is that extremism breeds extremism. At a benign level, unlikely relationships have sometimes developed between people commonly thought to be diehard opponents, such the friendship between Senator Edward Kennedy and Pastor Jerry Falwell. Constantly paired as the yin and the yang in staged-for-television confrontations, they each came to be the best fundraiser for the other, and in the end turned out to enjoy each other.

Such unlikely friendships are the rarer trend. More often the result of extremism is the repression of one side by the other, and in the end the return of the repressed with a vengeance—and thus a general escalation of extremism. Consider the often-discussed links between the repressive secularist-leaning regime of the CIA-supported Shah of Iran and the revolutionary theocracy of Ayatollah Khomeini, or the secularizing militancy of Madalyn Murray O'Hair and the rise of the Moral Majority, or the muscle-flexing of the religious right and the strident triumphalism of the new atheists. Extremists who oppose each other with no humility come to deserve each other, then grow like each other and in the end become living contradictions of their own position and the best arguments for all they stand against.

Is there an alternative to the deficiencies of the naked public square on one side and the sacred public square on the other? Or are we condemned to an endless repetition of their follies and injustices? My alternative is the constructive proposal for a civil public square, which is at the heart of this book in chapter eight. But before we turn to consider any proposed solution, we have to assess the full scale of the challenges we face, including an appraisal of the inadequacy of the two models and the extremism on both sides. Only then can we muster the courage to break with the stale patterns of a generation of culture warring and seek a new solution for the new challenges of the global era.

Again, it is time, and past time, to ponder the question. What does it say of us and our times that the Universal Declaration of Human Rights could not be passed today? And what does it say of the future of freedom of thought, conscience, religion and belief if it can be neglected and threatened even in the United States, where it once developed most fully—that it can be endangered anywhere? Who will step forward now to champion the cause of freedom for the good of all and for the future of humanity?

7

LOOKING IN
THE WRONG PLACE

THE SIXTH STEP IN THE REVALUATION *is to examine the weaknesses of many of the present responses to the problems of religion in public life, and to see why they will never succeed because they are looking for answers in the wrong place by disregarding the nature of freedom of thought and conscience.*

Goethe once observed that it is natural to look where there is light. The great Austrian satirist Karl Kraus played on this point in a famous sketch in which he played a drunk looking for his keys under a lamppost, although he had lost them elsewhere—there was more light under the lamppost, he said, than where he had lost them. In the same way, there are many people trying to solve the problems of religion and public life today who have no chance of success. However well intentioned and however determined, they are simply looking for answers where no answers will ever be found—and in doing so, they often make the problems worse.

Put differently, the simple requirement for finding solutions to the various problems of religion and public life is to get people to look for the answers in the right place, and to do so by respecting the character of both freedom and ultimate beliefs and therefore to see how freedom of thought, conscience, religion and belief can best be secured, expanded and sustained.

TONE-DEAF AT THE MUSIC FESTIVAL

One problem I have noted at several points is that those who disdain religion discount freedom of religion and belief. There are many reasons for this error, but a major one is the tone deafness of intellectuals who oppose any place for religion in public life because they presume religion is set to disappear from the modern world. With this presumption in mind, they do not see that their blind spot toward religion seriously distorts their vision, and their exclusion of religious voices in public life then makes them highly illiberal. Either way, they never take religion seriously enough to understand it on its own terms—to their own cost.

It was said that in the ten years prior to the Iranian revolution that overthrew the Shah's regime in 1979, there was only one American intelligence analysis that accurately predicted the rising power of the ayatollahs—and it was dismissed in one word: *sociology.* As one scholar explained later, the word was used to describe "the time-wasting study of factors deemed politically irrelevant"—principally religion.[1]

When the eminent journalist Abe Rosenthal reflected on more than fifty years of reporting for the *New York Times,* he wrote, "I realized that in decades of reporting, writing, or assigning stories on human rights, I rarely touched on the most important. Political, legal, civil and press rights, emphatically often; but the right to worship where and how God or conscience leads, almost never."[2]

The same lesson is plain in the appalling, long-running case of Pastor Youcef Nadarkhani. He was sentenced to death in Iran in 2009 for the apostasy of converting to the Christian faith and three times steadfastly refused to recant. He was then kept under sentence of death for nearly three years until he was released in 2012 after strong international protest—and then rearrested. Oddly, his case came to be championed by the White House, the British Foreign Office, France, the European Union and thousands of individuals long before it was picked up by Amnesty International and the Human Rights Watch—the human rights organizations who, by definition, should have been the ones to stand up for him from the start. Turkish writer Ziya Meral commented dryly, "You know something is really wrong when a major human rights group picks up on a human rights concern after governments, mainstream and social media do."[3]

The terms *tone deaf* and *unmusical* were made famous by Max Weber, who used them to describe the religious incomprehension of Western elites, but the comment goes back earlier still. The Jewish mystic Baal Shem Tov compared atheists to a deaf man encountering a fiddler playing in a town square with the locals dancing to the music with joy. Unable to hear anything he pronounces them all mad. Still others have compared such atheists to an angry landowner who banned all music on his estate because he could not bear not being able to hear it.

We all know that dogs, bats and bears can pick up sounds at frequency levels that we as humans cannot hear, but the fact that our ears do not hear the sounds does not make them unreal. The sounds are objectively real, but we are unable to pick them up. In a similar way, there are certain worldviews that predefine what is real and preselect how we are to discover it, and therefore pay no attention to realities that lie beyond their range. The advocates of such views are prisoners of their own limited expectations. The worldviews of the tone deaf are not only self-invented, as they so proudly boast, but self-enclosed and self-impaired.

It is true that with some of our modern technologies, we can see some things far more clearly than our ancestors—for example, the structure of biological cells or the details of craters on Mars. But it is also true that with some of our modern philosophies, there are other realities that we no longer see or hear at all. As Shakespeare's Hamlet says to his friend, "There are more things in heaven and earth, Horatio, than are dreamt of in your philosophy."[4]

One example of tone deafness is scientific materialism, whose advocates refuse to believe anything that reason cannot understand and science cannot verify as predictable and repeatable, and who therefore reduce everything to their own mechanistic world. Quite literally, they are reality-challenged. They forget that any system must be understood from outside the system, so that all self-contained rational systems are necessarily incomplete. If pressed consistently, systems of thought will always point beyond themselves. Thus science helps us to see many things in the world more easily and clearly than ever before, but scientific materialism hurts us because it then jumps to the conclusion that that is all there is to be seen.

Needless to say, scientific materialism is not the position of many of the greatest scientists. Max Planck, for instance, was humbler. "Anybody who has been seriously engaged in scientific work of any kind realizes that over the entrance to the gates of the temple of science are written the words: *Ye must have faith.* It is a quality which the scientist cannot dispense with." After all, "Science cannot solve the ultimate mystery of nature. And that is because, in the last analysis, we ourselves are part of nature and therefore part of the mystery we are trying to solve."[5]

Some atheists acknowledge their condition openly. The philosopher Isaiah Berlin first met Jonathan Sacks with the opening, "Chief Rabbi, what ever you do, don't talk to me about religion. When it comes to God, *I'm tone deaf!*" (He later asked him to officiate at his funeral.) Many secularists are like that, only less frank. Nonreligious themselves, they simply do not hear the music by which most people in the world orchestrate their lives. Color blind, they cannot see the beauty of the rainbows seen by others. More recently, several observers have criticized the U.S. State Department for its "blind spot" over religious factors (Paul Marshall), its "blinding secularity" (George Weigel), its "religious avoidance syndrome" and "lack of mosque time" (Thomas Farr), all of which have had such practical and avoidable consequences in American foreign policy.

Needless to say, the State Department does not stand alone in its tone deafness, and similar indictments could be handed down to many branches of the Civil Service in Europe as well as many university departments across the world. Peter Berger, astute observer of the religious scene and modern heir to Max Weber, once remarked that the real mystery is not the radical imams, who are readily explicable according to their beliefs, but the American professors who do not understand them. After all, Berger has long quipped: the United States is "a nation of Indians ruled by Swedes." Whereas ordinary Americans are as religious as the people of India, the most religious country in the world, educated Americans tend to be as secular as the people of Sweden, at that time the most secular country in the world.

Sometimes the malady of tone deafness has results that are comic, sometimes serious. It is remarkable, for instance, how often people who would be shocked if other people were denigrated for their race or gender, think nothing of insulting them on account of their religion. More often, the results are mild. The unmusical just don't get it, and both the impairment and the misfortune are theirs.

Where does this tone deafness come from? The worldview is the underlying problem and below that the dominance of left-brain thinking, as the chosen focus of attention limits the range of its perceptions. As the neurologists put it, the left brain delivers what we know rather than what we experience. Those, for example, who refuse to believe in anything that is not verifiable through science will never understand their own freedom or falling in love, let alone be able to experience God. Such things are beyond the frequency levels of their limited thinking. Heraclitus put the point tartly long ago, "He who does not expect will not find out the unexpected, for it is trackless and unexplored."[6]

WHO NOW IS THE ODD MAN OUT?

Beyond that basic limitation in worldviews, there are certain other powerful reinforcements in our world today. One is that many educated Westerners still subscribe unthinkingly to the secularization theory that came out of the French Enlightenment. Dominant for more than two hundred years and associated with such seminal thinkers as Auguste Comte, Émile Durkheim and Max Weber himself, the secularization theory is the idea that the more modern the world becomes, the less religious the world is becoming. Europe, then, was taken as the precedent, so that as Europe went, so also the world would eventually go. The United States was therefore the odd man out. It was considered exceptional as the most modern country in the world that was also the most religious of modern countries. In my student days it was commonplace to hear celebrated intellectuals such as Bertrand Russell and Arnold Toynbee pronounce that the days of religion were ebbing like the tide on Matthew Arnold's "Dover Beach"—the former rubbing it in with glee and the latter sighing with a weary sadness.

Needless to say, the recent resurgence of religion stunned the advocates of this theory into a drastic revision, though astute critics such as David Martin had challenged the theory even earlier. The secularization theory was shown up as factually wrong as well as philosophically biased. It was a clear case of Freudian wish fulfillment, in that many advocates of the theory had smuggled into it assumptions that supported the outcome, but ones which some of them expected for other reasons and still others desired.

As things stand now, it is clear that religion is anything but disappearing, that America is very much in line with most of the world, and that there are only two major exceptions. One is geographical—Europe, for historical European reasons, and the other is social—the educated classes, for more philosophical reasons.

In short, the tone deafness is explicable but inexcusable. And it reinforces how the tone deaf see reality: religion and religious believers are simply not behaving as the theory says they should. When all the expectations say they should be disappearing, their continued strength must be a symptom of their rage and irrationality.

For Americans in particular, a third reason for the tone deafness lies in a mythical understanding of their founders' notion of the separation of church and state. Originally a unique and decisive institutional separation of church and state, the founders' breakthrough in church-state affairs did not separate faith and public life and was never intended to. When he first used the term, Roger Williams had in mind the protection of the church from the state and not the other way around. What the principle summarily forbade for the American founders, a century later, was any official establishment of religion. In other words, the Establishment Clause was in the service of the Free Exercise Clause, and both were unambiguously in the service of freedom.

Thomas Jefferson, for example, was the American founder with the strongest version of the wall of separation, and he was both separationist and utilitarian in his views of religion in public life. For all the years that Jefferson was president, deist though he was, he was a regular attender at the largest church service in the United States—under the roof of the U.S. Capitol. He also invited Baptists and Episcopalians to hold worship services, including Holy Communion, in the executive branch buildings. A hero to the ACLU today, he would have offended the ACLU then—if there had been one.

Some say that his inconsistency was like his views on slavery, hypocritical, but it is far more likely that he was utilitarian and espoused an early form of what is now called "belonging without believing." Similarly, when Golda Meir was asked whether she believed in God, replied famously: "I believe in the Jewish people, and they believe in God."

What changed the founders' settlement beyond recognition was not the separation of church and state. Disestablishment was the genius of their settlement. The damaging change was the far more recent triumph of *strict separation* or *separationism* that came to the fore in *Everson v. Board of Directors* in 1947. According to the new view, and in sharp contrast to Jefferson and the founders, the "wall of separation" was to be "high and impregnable," religion was to be inviolably private, and the public square was to be strictly and inviolably secular. Thus was born an American-style *laïcité*.

The grand irony is that whereas the founders hoped the French revolution would copy the American, Americans intellectuals are now bent on copying the French and on producing what Richard John Neuhaus called the "naked public square." Promoted by ardent secularists, such as Madalyn Murray O'Hair, and quickly countered by equally ardent supporters of school prayer, such as the Moral Majority, this position has become one of the two poles in the holy war front of the emerging culture wars.

For most educated people this distorted understanding of the separation of church and state was raised to canonical status following the publication of John Rawls's *A Theory of Justice* in 1973. From then on until today, it is axiomatic for many people that faith, character and virtue have no place in the public square. The latter is a neutral arena of competing self-interests, where reason, law, science and technology all have their place, but not religion. The public square is inviolably secular, and religion is inviolably private.

The fourth and lesser factor in the tone deafness of the elites is the influence of the more recent movement that is loosely called postmodernism. Among its diverse and often contradictory ideas is the central Nietzschean theme, picked up by Michel Foucault, that truth is dead and claims to knowledge are really a bid for power. The result at the elite level is the infamous "hermeneutics of suspicion." At the street level the result is a massive groundswell of cynicism. Nothing is ever what it appears to be. Things are always other than they seem. Simple and straightforward reasons are really expressions of an underlying agenda and a push for power. There is never smoke without a smoke machine.

Today, the acid of postmodernism is corroding the strength of human rights both domestically and internationally. In a style worthy of Soviet-era communists, postmodern liberals (AKA *former* liberals) are routinely brushing aside sincere claims to the human rights of freedom of conscience and religious liberty with their own sneering explanations (AKA cynicism). Aha, they say, talk of religious freedom is not a straightforward claim to a human right. For as the knowing ones know well, it is really a code word for hidden agendas. At best the real agenda behind the believers' concern for the persecuted around the world is their fight for their "coreligionists" elsewhere and for "paving the way for missionaries" everywhere. At worst the true endgame of the rhetoric of religious freedom is "promoting a higher role for religion in American national life" or providing a cosmetic cover for all their positions of "bigotry and intolerance."

With such postliberals in full cry, all human rights and even freedom itself are at risk. Human rights are now dismissible at a postmodern whim, so their universality is in question. There is no objective standard to appeal to in order to escape the cynical eye of elite opinion, so no claims to rights are listened to on their own terms, and the weak and unfashionable are at risk. Claims that pass muster before the opinions that count will be deemed rights. Claims that fail to pass muster need not even be debated. They can simply be dismissed out of hand as unacceptable intolerance.

As with all skepticism, the trouble for such skeptics comes when the postmodern sword descends on the cherished beliefs of its wielders too, and few things are as pathetic as the sight of the relativizer relativized. Witness, for instance, the sorry end of A. J. Ayer's verification principle.

Fortunately, however, such rigid intolerance has not yet won the day. In fact, we are now seeing encouraging cracks in the ice age that had begun to freeze and form the naked public square for the last half-century. And ironically, the thaw is beginning not in "religious America" but in "secular Europe." Philosopher Jürgen Habermas, who is as influential in Europe as John Rawls is in the United States, is arguing strongly that to exclude diverse religious voices from the public square is both illiberal as a denial of democracy and an impoverishment of public life.

Tone deafness stands as the major reason for the incomprehension of educated opinion in dealing with religious issues—which is another way of saying that many educated people are uneducated when it comes to religion and religious issues. Beyond this, however, lie two other trends that are massive obstacles to resolving the troubled questions of religion and public life: the problem of the unconservative actions of many conservatives and the illiberal actions of many liberals.

Both these trends are damaging for the nations in which they are allowed to grow. But curiously, they hurt no one more than conservatives and liberals themselves. For when conservatives act unconservatively, they provoke revulsion against the faith that is their heart and soul, just as when liberals act illiberally they undermine the freedom that is their raison d'être.

JUSTICE, NOT JUST US

There are two significant ways in which many conservatives now act unconservatively in fighting back against what they see as violations of freedom of religion and belief, and both are examples of looking for answers in the wrong place. The first is to defend freedom of religion and belief by defending only their own interests rather than those of the common good. Commenting on the Religious Right in the 1980s, a journalist said to me, "They talk justice, but what they really mean is 'just us.'"

Such self-interested partisanship is ideal for culture warring, but a liability in addressing issues that are for the good of all and in the interests of humanity and justice, and eventually it creates a backlash against the freedom defended. On the one hand, faith has always been most beneficial and progressive in public life when it addresses the common good and calls on a moral inspiration that transcends political divisions—as in the movement to abolish slavery and in civil rights. On the other hand, when religious freedom is pressed in a culture warring style or in the thick of an election campaign, the impression given is that freedom of thought and conscience is purely partisan and a matter of self-interest—and therefore to be opposed or ignored by the other side.

Neither the selfishness nor the selectiveness in limiting rights is new. In *Areopagitica*, John Milton's clarion cry for freedom in 1689, he cried out boldly, "Give me the liberty to know, to utter, and to argue freely according to conscience, above all liberties." But unlike Roger Williams, he advocated freedom for all dissenters, but he did not include Roman Catholics. Similarly, John Locke advocated a strong view of toleration that has made him a hero of toleration ever since, but that praise should be qualified because he did not include either Catholics or atheists. Mary Dyer, the Quaker who was hanged in Boston for her beliefs, came up against such limits and paid for them with her life. For the Puritans of the Bay Colony, it was "religious freedom for me, but not for thee."[7]

Rights without responsibilities, an exaggerated sense of entitlement, an insistence on interpreting rights only within the framework of a self-absorbed individualism, and a selective application of rights have all become serious problems in the Western world. Either such attitudes give the impression that rights are culturally relative, for some and not for others, or—in an Orwellian twist—they seem to suggest that all rights are equal, but some are more equal than others.

This in turn opens the door for authoritarian religions and totalitarian ideologies to claim that human rights are Western and ethnocentric, and then either to reject them altogether as alien and imposed, or to press for their own form of rights from within their own ideology or religion. There is truth behind this accusation. In 1933, for example, a Haitian diplomat argued that states should protect the rights of everybody and not just the minorities that were then under discussion. A British official remarked in response that "he did not wish to be quoted," but "the acceptance of such a proposal by His Majesty's Government would be entirely impossible in view of our colonial experience."[8]

Such selectivity, also known as hypocrisy, is quite wrong, but it does not justify further selectivity on the other side. In 1990 the Cairo Declaration, for instance, put forward an Islamic view of rights, but one that on closer reading had to be understood within the framework of the Qur'an and obviously favored Islam at the expense of all other faiths. "Everyone should have the right to express his opinion freely," it declared in effect, but then took back what it had just offered when it added, "in such manner as would not be contrary to the principles of the Shari'a." Speak freely and say whatever you like, but only if you say what we like and we like what you say.

A subtler version of the same tactic is the Tehran Declaration and Programme of Action (2007). With greater sophistication in political correctness, it argues for cultural diversity. But it then uses the concept to call for the banning of anything deemed offensive to the ruling majority in the culture whose diversity was to be guarded—namely, Muslims. Cultural diversity trumps universality. If such deficient views prevail, they would be a heavy blow to the universality of human rights, which in turn would provide ammunition to the enemies of human rights from both secularist and religious extremes. Unless checked and corrected, such selfish individualism and selectivity acts to undermine all human rights and the human rights revolution itself.

Soul freedom, however, points in a different direction. As a right rooted in the nature of the human person, freedom of thought, conscience, religion and belief is automatically a right of belonging, and therefore assumes and requires the respect of all the other people in the same community, society and the world itself. Indeed, the Marquis de Condorcet pointed out the inclusive logic of rights: "He who votes against the rights of another . . . has thereby abjured his own."[9]

As I have said repeatedly, we are talking of soul freedom for all. A right for one person or group is a right for another and a responsibility for both. There are no solo rights and no Robinson Crusoe claims, so there are no rights that are not immediately and automatically the rights of all others too. "My rights" are always also "our rights," so my rights depend on your rights, just as your rights depend on my rights, so that together we have a duty and we owe a debt in relation to the claims of others, just as they owe the same to us. Liberty must always walk hand in hand with solidarity and with reciprocity.

It is often noted that the Golden Rule or its negative version, the Silver Rule, is shared by many of the world's religions and is perhaps the most nearly universal ethic in human history. When a disciple asked Confucius if his rule of conduct could be summed up in a single word, the Master replied: "Is not 'reciprocity' the word?"[10] That by itself should be enough to underscore the mutuality and reciprocity of human rights. No right is an individual right alone. It is a shared right. A right for one is a right for another and a responsibility for both. As Jefferson wrote, "When arguing for ourselves, we lay it down as fundamental, that laws, to be just, must give a reciprocation of right: that, without this, they are mere arbitrary rules of conduct, founded in force, and not in conscience."[11]

Shame, then, on the people of Switzerland, who in an open violation of freedom of religion and belief, voted in 2009 to forbid the construction of minarets within their borders. But shame too on the leaders of Saudi Arabia who give millions for the construction of mosques all around the world, yet forbid the building of churches and other religious buildings within their own kingdom (among their many violations of religious freedom).

Besides the principle of reciprocity, certain communities of faith should be concerned for others as a matter of their own principles and therefore have an ever-eager eye for the common good and especially for the stranger and the oppressed. Jesus of Nazareth, it has often been said, was "a man for others," just as the Christian church has been described as "a club for nonmembers of the club." For Christians, then, to stand, or be thought to stand, only for their own rights is not only counterproductive but egregiously wrong and hypocritical.

Beyond such considerations for individual faiths, there is the general challenge of the nature of freedom of thought and conscience. Soul freedom is such that each person and each group must realize that their own rights are best protected when the rights of all others are protected too, and that the real test of freedom of thought and conscience for all is when the rights of the smallest community and the most unpopular community are just as respected as the rights of the powerful and the fashionable. Article 9 of the Global Charter of Conscience declares:

The right to freedom of thought, conscience, and religion contains a duty as well as a right, an obligation and not only an entitlement, because a right for one person is automatically a right for another and a responsibility for both. All citizens are responsible for the rights of all other citizens, just as others are responsible for theirs. A society is only as just and free as it is respectful of this right, especially toward the beliefs of its smallest minorities and least popular communities.

In short, a preoccupation with "me, myself and I" may be a perfect expression of the logic of Western individualism. But it is a shrunken conservative view of rights just as freedom of worship is a shrunken liberal view of rights. It is a dire contradiction of human rights as well as the Golden Rule and the ethical teaching of many of the world's great faiths. Freedom of thought and conscience is responsible, mutual and universal, and carries a duty to the common good, the good of everyone. In the global era more than ever, there is no avoiding that we are our brothers' and our sisters' keepers. Our rights depend on their rights too, and the surest way to protect our rights is to ensure theirs first.

In 1860 on the eve of the American Civil War, Francis Wayland, president of Brown University in Rhode Island, captured the revolutionary feature of Roger Williams's stand that must be an essential feature of all human rights today. The Puritans had come seeking freedom for themselves, but Roger Williams had sought "liberty for humanity."[12] And so today should we.

LAW VERSUS HABITS OF THE HEART

The second way in which conservatives are acting unconservatively is when they fight on behalf of freedom of religion and belief through law and litigation alone—in other words, when they forget the place of customs, traditions and civic education, which Alexis de Tocqueville aptly called the "habits of the heart." From classical authors such as Polybius and Cicero to more modern authors such as Montesquieu and Tocqueville, not to speak of the American founders and their "golden triangle of freedom," there was a strong consensus that freedom and justice are protected by the bulwark of law but guaranteed most firmly when they are also cultivated as a second nature and a habit of the heart.[13]

In Montesquieu's terms, liberty depends not only on the *structures* of liberty, such as a constitution, but on the *spirit* of liberty, which must be kept alive in the hearts of citizens and passed from generation to generation through civic education. Indeed, contrary to current thinking, the spirit of liberty is even more vital than the structures of liberty, for the structures provide only the setting for free people, whereas the spirit of liberty is the vital impulse that makes free people free. Nations can pass laws until their statute books can take no more, but their societies will only be free and their peoples will only live freely if they believe in freedom, know what freedom is and isn't, and know how to treasure freedom of thought, conscience, religion and belief in practice.

Not so today. For much of the Western world, human rights are synonymous with law and even more with laws. Mention a particular freedom or right and some one will tell you the laws, articles, statutes and conventions in which it is expressed. Liberty and legality have become equated. The law *is* the human right, and it no longer requires any philosophical or moral conviction behind it, of which the law is the legal expression. The result is a simultaneous rush to law and a shrinking of freedom.

This serious mistake has become important in different parts of the world for different reasons. In Europe it matters because religious freedom is now anchored in the constitutions and laws of many countries, but not in the hearts of the citizenry. Such was the prestige of the Universal Declaration that it quickly led to laws being put in place across Europe, but in many cases their force is theoretical only. They have little binding address on the average citizen, and will never have authority or credibility unless there is civic education to match the laws, and effective civic education that turns liberty into a sturdy habit of the heart.

In America the point is vital too because things have changed since Tocqueville used the phrase *habits of the heart* to describe Americans and the secret of American freedom. Among other things, there has been a general secularization of American life; a serious diminishing of any civic education; an overall rush to the rhetoric of rights, claims and entitlements; a determined push by secular elites to exclude religion from public life; and a pronounced swing toward creating a secularist state orthodoxy. In short, the habits of the American heart are almost threadbare.

To be sure, Tocqueville also observed that in the United States all political questions eventually become judicial questions, and since Tocqueville, lawyer-think and legalisms have pervaded America from top to bottom. But he was also emphatic that what mattered finally for freedom was not the law but the habits of the heart. Seen one way, all roads in America lead to the Supreme Court. But seen another way, when the habits of the heart are healthy, fewer roads should ever have to leave their local region. When the habits of the heart are strong, law need have less prominence and can afford to be less extensive and intrusive. In Samuel Johnson's famous words, "How small of all that human hearts endure / That part which laws or kings can cause or cure."[14]

The wisdom of this insistence has recently been abandoned under the impact of three powerful twentieth-century trends: the relentless expansion of the state, the general secularization of Western life since the 1920s, and the rise of a culture of rights, claims and entitlement. In her superb study *Rights Talk*, Mary Ann Glendon argues that America has become the "land of rights," and

"Americans today, for better or worse, live in what is undoubtedly one of the most law-ridden societies on the face of the earth."[15]

The result is ironic. The constant pursuit of rights through law alone rather than the habits of the heart has caught Americans in the toils of ever-spreading law. On the one hand, it has led to a strengthening of the law at the expense of the habits of the heart, of litigation at the expense of both civic education and the role of parents and schools, and of the lawyers and the lawyer class at the expense of other public servants. Just cross the street in Washington, DC, and you run the risk of tripping over a lawyer or a lobbyist scurrying about the business of finding a loophole in an existing law or drafting a new law to favor their client's interests.

Unless deliberately checked, the situation in both Europe and America can only deteriorate. Once free to do whatever was not forbidden, we will soon be free to do only what we are told are the rights given to us—and given to us, of course, by the ever-caring and ever-expanding state.

On the other hand, the pursuit of rights through law has also led to a marked weakening of law in the face of the expanding state, so that the state can always find a thousand ways around the laws designed to restrain it. Columnist George Will protests this bloating of the law: "As the regulatory state's micromanagement of society metastasizes, inconvenient laws are construed—by those the laws are supposed to restrain—as porous and permissive, enabling the executive branch to render them nullities."[16] The expanding state begins by thickening the web of laws, and then ends by brushing them aside as cobwebs. Thus the more powerful the state, the more numerous but weaker the laws, and the loser is always freedom.

After all, if the modern state is regarded as the author of rights, and the individual is liable to be set over against the general will, then two things will always follow. On the one hand, it is the role of the beneficent state to help us each realize our rights to the fullest as it generously decides to dole them out to us. On the other hand, the logic leads directly to Jean Jacques Rousseau's infamous paradox concerning the citizen: "This means nothing less than that he will be *forced to be free.*"[17]

The final irony in this constant resort to law, to judges, to the ever-adjudicating state and to ever-expanding regulations should be plain to all with eyes to see. *These are the very people and these are the very institutions from which human rights were designed to free us in the first place.* The paradox of freedom strikes again: freedom becomes its own worst enemy.

This disastrous shift away from the habits of the heart might be expected from those who favor the expanded state, but not from conservatives who should have respected the earlier traditions and tried to keep such habits alive in order to keep law and government at bay. Back in the 1980s an ACLU leader said to me smugly, "There is a simple reason why we will always win the culture wars—we have more lawyers than anyone else." Today, a generation later, that is no longer true. Liberal lawyers, liberal defense funds and liberal litigation are meeting their match in conservative lawyers, conservative defense funds and conservative litigation—and the result is the bitter, polarized stalemate of the American culture wars and signs of the beginnings of the same in Europe.

Let there be no misunderstanding. Law, the rule of law, the due process of law and constitutionalism are essential, vital and precious protections of freedom. It is not the business of governments to prescribe for free people their moral principles or to oversee that they choose wisely. But the genuine liberty of free people can only flourish within wise limits that are clearly known and steadily enforced, and that is the importance of the rule of law.

Sir Edward Coke, Roger Williams's patron and England's greatest legal advocate for freedom under law gave his friends a ring engraved with the motto *Lex est tuti cassis* (Law is the safest helmet).

This fundamental principle is best preserved in the work of organizations such as the Becket Fund, Christian Solidarity Worldwide and the International Justice Mission, which work tirelessly to defend the rights of thought, conscience, religion and belief for people of all faiths and none.

But that said, let it be understood equally clearly: By itself, law is never enough to protect and promote freedom.

- First, law alone is too blunt an instrument to decide the many subtleties of the issues of religion and public life. Law can never be a total theory that answers all questions, resolves all issues and reconciles all conflicts. (Witness the drunken zigzagging of the U.S. Supreme Court in its attempts to do this, or ponder the simple fact that an ounce of civility would solve a ton of controversies that no litigation will ever help.)

- Second, reliance on law alone will lead only to mounting litigiousness and to an avalanche of laws and regulations that will stifle rather than stimulate freedom. This process is already well advanced, as every mass murder is routinely followed only by calls for greater gun control and every banking scandal only by fresh inquiries into ever-tighter regulations and ever-stricter compliance.

- And third, the law is always the state speaking, so that whatever the law passed is, the state always expands behind it. And in addition there is always a tendency for some faction to use law to promote their factional interests at the expense of the freedom of thought, conscience and religion that should lie beyond the reach of the law.

The last point deserves special reflection. We who prize democracy must never forget that the corruption of democracy has produced tyranny and terror before—most notably, in Athens, Paris and Weimar. After all, it was democrats and not oligarchs who sentenced Socrates to death, just as it was the popular revolution in France that ushered in the reign of terror. Even Adolf Hitler could claim a democratic majority at the beginning of his rise to power, and he rose in reaction to the corruptions of Weimar liberalism.

Behind such precedents stands a cautionary principle: the power of a democratic people needs to be checked and balanced just as much as the power of the king. Indeed, such is the force of an unsatisfied people that no dictator is more dangerous than one who takes over power in order to fulfill their insatiable demands.

It has been argued, most famously by Thomas Hobbes, that at a certain point of chaos only the monarch or the state can intervene and bring order rather than allow a war of all against all between the citizens—or in a more recent example, that the United States should not pull its army out of Iraq in 2007 or the country would descend into chaos. But that argument can be turned on its head, and it can be countered that it is precisely when the overreaching state "liberates" citizens from their proper responsibilities, usurps the place of the local community and debases citizens into being mere individuals, clients and statistics, that the state fosters the conditions in which individual humans will act as wolves to other humans (Hobbes's *homo homini lupus*)—or in the case of Iraq, that it was precisely the manner of the invasion of Iraq that destroyed the Iraqi state and created the chaos that the U.S. army found itself inadequate to deal with.

Was the future of America itself prefigured in the fate of Iraq after the American invasion? Time will tell. Freedom of thought and conscience was once won against the power of kings and emperors. It reminded them that they too were "under God." It was true that no monarch could be under any mere man, for he would then be subject to his own subjects. But the power of the monarch was still not absolute or final, for he was under God. In the words of Henry de Bracton, the great English scholar of the century of Magna Carta, *Quod Rex non debet esse sub homine, sed sub Deo et Lege* (the king should not be under man, but under God and the laws).[18]

Today's secularists have excised "under God" as a term said to be only a pious rhetorical flourish, a historical leftover and an affront to the nonreligious (and a red rag to the antireligious). They little realize that ever since the irruption into history of Jewish monotheism, "under God" has been the ultimate limit to the pretensions of power, so what they have removed is the final check and balance against all absolutism. For Jews and Christians, all human power is circumscribed: It can never be other than derived, limited, accountable and transient. It is always under God.

In today's world the power of the modern state has replaced the power of the king, so the struggle for freedom has to be won against the power of the state, and now even against the liberal state. Indeed, Lord Acton's "All power corrupts" is as true of the liberal state as the totalitarian state, of Europe and the United States as much as China and Cuba.

But in the West now, the modern state, unlike the king, is no longer said to be under God and therefore has little or nothing to check its power. Hence the rise of what Tocqueville warned as "soft despotism," but modern critics such as Jonathan Sacks and George Weigel have variously called "totalitarian democracy," the "libertine police state" and "soft totalitarianism"—the systematic attempt to eliminate the vital role played by the institutions of civil society "unless those institutions become the extension of the state" and its all-embracing will.[19]

In most Western democracies there is now no power higher or stronger than the state, and no moral limits to its power. So the law, speaking as the state, which in turn can be made to speak as the voice and arm of minority interests, has become the real menace to human rights in general and freedom of thought and conscience in particular. What is now looming is nothing less than the specter of liberal authoritarianism, for in general it is liberals who have the position, the resources and the vision to be able to command the powers of the state and its laws. There is now no end to what the law can be used to promote.

Make no mistake: the menace of the potential tyranny of the modern state can never be resisted successfully by a resort to law alone, and for conservatives to try to do so is double folly.

It was once a maxim of English constitution principles that "the king cannot die." This did not mean that any individual king had found the secret of eternal life, but that one king's death automatically meant the accession of the new king. "The King is dead. Long live the King!" In the same way today, it has almost become a principle of the modern state that "the government never shrinks"— even under smaller-government conservatives such as Ronald Reagan. Freedom of thought, conscience, religion and belief once served to rein in kings, and no monarch in the West today is now a threat to anyone. But the new king, the modern liberal state, is another matter, and if the liberal state continues to disregard any right, where is the standard to which we can appeal against this new ultimate power?

Yet at such a time activists and culture warriors, many of them conservatives, are riding roughshod over this insight with their fear mongering, alarmism, partisan appeals—and their hasty resort to law alone. The result is a deepening crisis of freedom of thought, conscience, religion and belief, reinforced in part by those who would defend it. As we shall see in chapter eight, civility properly understood can solve problems the law will never reach, and it is time for all who love freedom to pause and survey where the recent reliance on law and litigation alone is leading the world. Once again it is clear that freedom of thought and conscience, with its constant need for the oxygen of the habits of the heart, lies in a different direction and will never be protected by law alone.

Those who are intoxicated with the passion to turn every disagreement into an occasion for a lawsuit should ponder a simple point that will soon be duplicated across the rights-respecting world. There is a yawning chasm between the sublime simplicity of the first sixteen words of the First Amendment to the U.S. Constitution and the sprawling jungle of legal decisions it has grown. Laws will always beget more laws, but when there is no reliance on checks and balances of the habits of the heart, that toxic tendency can only spread like a cancer and kill the freedom of our free societies.

FIGHT THE NEGATIVE WITH THE POSITIVE

If conservative activists too often act unconservatively, liberal activists can act illiberally too. Two striking tendencies toward illiberalism are especially prominent today. The first comes when liberals fight for liberty in ways that are purely negative, when what the situation needs is a potent dose of the positive. This mistake is dangerous in itself, but it also creates an opening for the disastrous convergence between misguided liberal views and misguided Islamic views.

Take the recent vogue for regulating speech and sensitivity, or protesting against it with vigilante action. For classical liberals and all true lovers of freedom, it is sad but unquestionable that regulations against hate speech in the West have been used as the functional equivalent of blasphemy in the Muslim world. A kinder, gentler version perhaps, but just as wrong in principle and often damaging in practice. To be sure, there is a difference in the visions of the sacred that are offended—Allah for the followers of the Prophet and various current sacred cows for liberals more recently.

The fundamental and unavoidable problem with hate speech is that no one can say definitively what it is. The result is that there are huge and consequential differences between the claims, and since it is essentially subjective, it is always open to abuse. *To define hate speech according to the eye of the beholder is to put a sword in the hands of the power wielder.*

Problems created by speech are unquestionably serious, for any attack on the racial or religious identity of another is an attack on their humanity and the humanity of their group. Plus, there are countries such as the United States where race will always be especially sensitive due to the background history of slavery and the later "separate but equal" apartheid of the Jim Crow era. But what is true of race is not true of religion in America, and it might be argued that today's misplaced hypersensitivity toward religion is causing rather than solving the problem.

Besides, it should be the unshakable conviction of liberals that true freedom of speech always includes the right to speak in ways that are hateful. So the real question is how best to counter such hateful speech, how to prevent all forms of incivility and so to guard against any real hatred that may lie behind them.

Is it the case that hypersensitivity, regulations and policing are the best way to counter hate speech? Far from it. There are numerous pitfalls down that road. Sometimes an overzealous concern can lead to a tailoring of discourse and a self-censorship that excludes words deemed incorrect or offensive to certain groups. So the *New York Times* can offer a lengthy, explanatory article on Nigeria's Islamist terrorist group Boko Haram without a single reference to the meaning of its name (Western education is a sacrilege), to their goal (reimposing Sharia law on Nigeria) or to their recurring target (the cleansing of Christians from their region).[20] But what has journalism come to when plain truth is considered offensive?

Similarly, in 2008 the U.S. State Department and the Department of Homeland Security forbade their employees, including U.S. diplomats, to use the words such as *jihadist, Salafi, Wahhabist* or *ca-*

liphate for fear of offending Muslims, despite the accuracy of the words in many cases. In Britain the same year, the Home Secretary began to use the term *anti-Islamic activity* instead of *Islamic terrorism*, while the next year the U.S. Homeland Security raised the Orwellian stakes higher still. *Islamic terrorism* disappeared from government rhetoric and *manmade disasters* took its place. Easy oil money has unquestionably muted if not bought off large swathes of research and debate, but there are also well-known scholars in prestigious universities who are unable to speak their minds on Islam for fear of their lives.[21]

At other times the same overzealous concern results in penalizing people for "hate" and "hate speech," an approach that has entered public discourse on the back of politically correct thinking. This problem is bad enough in itself because hate is a subjective assessment. One person's honest disagreement can easily be made into another person's hate, and sooner or later the result is bound to be bullying and intimidation.

In 2012 it was quickly clear that the outbreak of anti-Americanism that greeted the amateurish and badly made video *Innocence of Muslims* was not about blasphemy, it was about politics and power—power using the pretext of blasphemy to stir long-simmering rage and resentment against American and Western dominance in world affairs. It was no accident that the "spontaneous" attack on the U.S. embassy in Libya just "happened" to break out on the anniversary of September 11.

The same abuse of power is true of hate speech too. It has become a leading tool to silence disagreements and opposition, but it always ends in stifling freedom itself. Follow the precarious fate of free speech in the two countries that were once its greatest champions—England and America. In Britain the Incitement to Religious Hatred Bill as originally drafted would have imposed a jail sentence on anyone convicted of saying anything deemed to have stirred up religious hatred. In America similar concerns surrounded the U.S. Hate Crimes Bill. Sponsored by champions of liberalism, such as the late Senator Ted Kennedy, it prescribes severe penalties for those committing crimes for religious reasons.

In both countries, there is deep concern about the chilling of free speech and the illiberalism of such liberalism. Where are Tom Paine and John Stuart Mill when we need them? Like the road to hell, the road to intimidation is paved with good intentions.

NEW TOOL FOR BULLIES

But that is not the end of the problem, for subjective notions such as hate speech have in turn aggravated two other negative responses: victim playing and phobiaization. The first of these bad responses occurs when people feel threatened and then play the victim card in order to seize the high ground by posing as "more victimized than thou." This tactic works well, of course, in societies influenced by the Jewish and Christian faiths, for as Nietzsche recognized with scorn, the latter privilege the status of the victim. Under some philosophies and in some cultures they would be treated simply as history's roadkill. Needless to say, hate speech itself is a crime viewed from the perspective of the victim rather than society, so the encouragement to victim playing grows out easily from the category.

There are two varieties of victim playing at work today. The mild version plays the victim role in a passive form and owes much to the guilt and shock of Western responses to the malignant evils of the Nazi death camps and the power of "Never again." Effective in the short run, this version of victim playing is counterproductive for its proponents in the long run because those who portray themselves as victims come to perceive themselves as victims and end by paralyzing themselves as victims.

The strong version is more militant and plays the victim role in an active form, for as Nietzsche also recognized, victimhood is the dangerous breeding ground of resentment. Consciously or not, radical Muslims are playing this card with abandon and milking for all their worth such grievances as colonialism, Islam's long failure to adapt to modernity and various purported outrages against their faith today. This leads to the highly organized redress rage of the Muslims, who react to perceived insults through "spontaneous" expressions of outrage and violence that are carefully organized and coordinated to invite Western apologies and induce Western appeasement. Such responses are of course political rather than religious and have more to do with power than faith. The notorious burning of the Qur'an by Pastor Terry Jones was therefore doubly foolish, providing Islamist radicals with another excuse for rage and murder as well as demonstrating yet again the anti-Christian methods of many Christian activists.

The second bad response is the more recent one that has become the new tool for bullies—phobiaization. *Phobiaization* is the clumsy term that describes how all disagreements and criticisms can be turned back on one's opponents by portraying them as products of the opponent's phobia. Thus group after group is now encouraged to retaliate against any and all criticisms by calling their critics "phobic." All disagreements with homosexuals are "homophobic," all criticisms of Muslims and Islam are "Islamophobic" and all attacks on Christians and the church are "Christophobic" or "Christianaphobic." In August 2010 *Time* magazine's cover story asked the question "Is America Islamophobic?"

There is no question that speech is a vital consideration for all who wish to promote freedom, that those who speak with hatred are a deadly menace to society and that censorship always arises at the hands of those who set themselves up as guardians of the community's moral standing—be they conservative as in the past or liberal as so often today. But for all the good intentions behind the policing of offense and the politics of hate speech, the unintended consequences are disastrous. For liberals who have introduced so much of the politically correct speech as well as the hate speech regulations on campuses, the hate crime bills in the British Parliament and the U.S. Congress, and the hate cases before the European Court of Human Rights, the result is the chilling of robust, tough-minded liberal debate.

If ever there was a need for plain speaking and truth telling, it is now when core freedoms are endangered. Instead, the stifling blanket of "No offense" wraps around our heads, potential charges of partiality are like concealed tripwires for our arguments and the fear of lawsuits, countersuits and even death threats and bounties hang over us like a sword.

It is sometimes asked why Christians are mocked and marginalized in ways that Muslims and other religions are not, and why Christians do not riot like Muslims when Jesus is depicted negatively in films such as Martin Scorsese's *The Last Temptation of Christ*; in art such as Andres Serrano's photograph *Piss Christ*, in which a crucifix is immersed in the artist's urine; or in staged productions such as *Jerry Springer: The Opera*. There are plainly double standards at play, and as Timothy Garton Ash reminds us, "Double standards are the warning signs of a free society."[22]

To speak plainly, the main reason for the double standards is the Muslim threat of violence. As the director general of the BBC acknowledged, "'I complain in the strongest possible terms,' is different from 'I complain in the strongest possible terms and I'm loading my AK47 as I write.'"[23]

There are other reasons for the double standards too, and not all of them are complimentary to Christians, who have earned a good part of the abuse heaped on them today. But two of the deepest reasons are simple yet profound, and also more positive.

First, phobiaization is a form of identity politics in which groups define themselves by whatever offends them. For in little more than a generation, Western society has gone from a culture of "no offense," where a mealy mouthed niceness softened all sharp distinctions, to a culture of "all offense," where anything and everything can be cited by the hypersensitive as offensive or "dissing" in some way or another.

Christians, however, should never be defined by what offends them, by what they are against, by the insults thrown at them or by any cultural insecurity. Followers of Jesus are just that, followers of Jesus, and their identity should therefore be defined by Jesus and by the way of life to which he called them. To anyone tempted to play the victim card, Eleanor Roosevelt used to offer a bracing reminder: "No one can make you feel inferior without your own consent."

Second, and following on from that, Jesus bluntly called those who wished to follow him to "deny themselves and take up their cross daily and follow me"—including bearing the offense of the scandal of the cross itself (Lk 9:23). That entry cost is at the heart of the Christian faith and an inescapable part of its way of life. First through the incarnation and then through the crucifixion, the God whom Christians follow is no stranger to prejudice, insults, false accusations and wrongful arrest, and those who follow him must be prepared for the same treatment too. Attacks on any individual or group should never diminish them if they know who they are and why. Indeed, such attacks betray the attacker by revealing the roots of their bitterness or bigotry.

So for Christians to descend to playing the power game of phobiaization—for power game is what it is—violates their faith in a manner worse than any violation against them. To a people whose worship centers on a man spread-eagled, naked and in excruciating pain on an executioner's instrument of torture and death, it should be clear that defamation and even hate are par for the course, and never the grounds for pleading victimhood or arguing that opponents are guilty of Christophobia. Christians, in sum, are called to be broad shouldered, for the strength it takes to carry the cross is the same strength it takes to bear any and all insults and assaults that will come with it.

Sadly, the Russian Orthodox Church stands apart from most Christian traditions today in refusing to appreciate this point. Abandoning its own magnificent tradition of the holy fool, the person who counts it a joy to bear the folly of the world at any time, the Russian Church has followed in the steps of the czars and radical Islam rather than the way of Jesus. In 2012 the Church was quick to react to the Pussy Riot "punk prayer" ("Birthgiver of God, drive away Putin") in Moscow's Cathedral of the Savior. They pushed a bill through the Russian Parliament, criminalizing blasphemy and imposing long prison sentences and high fines on the feminists—all with the overwhelming support of the Russian people and in the interests of defending their monopoly position in Russian society. Needless to say, this Orthodox reaction was using the cross as a club to defend their power rather than as a badge of shame that was to be worn with pride.

Equally clearly, many Muslims concur with the Russian Orthodox Church and are attempting to exploit their religion and their cultural situation to the full. They desire to advance their faith by playing such negative cards as *insults* and *defamation* to the Prophet, *blasphemy* to Allah and *apostasy* to Islam. More particularly, their strategy is to promote their cause through the world by taking a misguided Western notion and turning it back on the West itself and on freedom of thought, conscience and religion in particular. This has long been the strategy of the Saudi-based Organization of the Islamic Conference (OIC), to which more than fifty countries now belong. It has worked hard to influence the United Nations General Assembly and the U.N. Council on

Human Rights and pass a legally binding ban on any perceived defamation of religion.

Little wonder that liberals, with their own concern for speech sensitivity, were initially vulnerable to the Muslim strategy. Indeed, uncertain of their own position on religious freedom and under the pressure of Muslim interest groups, they have given it a hearing, even at the highest government levels. But fortunately this dangerous Muslim strategy has so far been rebuffed and strenuously needs to be rejected altogether.

There is a comic contradiction between the liberal drive to throw out all anti-Christian blasphemy laws and at the same time to kowtow to Muslim attempts to introduce new ones. But that is not the real problem. The deadly danger at the heart of this liberal folly is the aiding and abetting of a deliberate attempt to cut the heart out of the first two core human rights—freedom of conscience and freedom of speech. The OIC tactic parallels the liberals' own notions of regulating discourse and policing hate speech. But as liberals are beginning to realize to their chagrin, the consequences are illiberal and a disaster for human rights and freedom.

- First, the Muslim tactic undercuts the long and important tradition that freedom of conscience protects *believers* rather than *beliefs*, and in particular protects *all* believers, inclusively and indiscriminately, rather than one favored belief: Islam. Plainly, the term *defamation of religions* is a code word for outlawing criticism of Islam and thus is a brazen attempt to overturn more than two centuries of protection for individual rights that includes the Bill of Rights and the Universal Declaration of Human Rights.

- Second, studies of earlier evils such anti-Semitism demonstrate that hate-speech prosecutions have not achieved what their authors hoped to achieve. Rather, such restrictions leave the universities and countries that adopt them more litigious, uncertain and restless than ever, and vulnerable to even greater tensions and conflict.[24]

• Third, the Muslim tactic puts a dangerous weapon in the hands of governments, imams, terrorists, mobs and vigilantes alike. The result is a license to bully, intimidate and oppress. Accuse someone of defamation and blasphemy, or declare anyone an apostate, and they can be arrested, imprisoned, tortured and killed at will—or as Salman Rushdie can attest, at the drop of a *fatwa*.

In an appalling case in 2012 near Islamabad, the capital of Pakistan, Rimsha Masih, an eleven-year-old girl, a street sweeper and reportedly shy and suffering from learning disabilities, was arrested and jailed along with her mother for allegedly desecrating some pages of the Qur'an. At first it was thought that she perhaps had swept up the pages inadvertently with her broom. Would she be lynched by the mob, sentenced to death or face a lifetime in prison? Would her home be burned down around her and her family as the mob threatened? Her father feared for her life and for the safety of the entire family, and many other Christian families fled the area immediately.

But then, as if to illustrate how insidious blasphemy laws are (and the quasi-blasphemy laws of Western hate speech), and how they can be manipulated with ease, the local imam was arrested for planting the pages, and it was said that the pages were not from the Qur'an at all but from a religious textbook for children. According to a witness, Imam Khalid Chishti told his deputy that he had added the pages to the girl's bag. "You know this is the only way to expel the Christians from this area."[25]

This case is only one of thousands in Pakistan, but it proves beyond a shadow of a doubt that it is not the misuse and abuse of the blasphemy laws that is wrong, as the U.S. State Department piously responded to the early reports. It is their very existence, and Western leaders should say so with unequivocal clarity. The blasphemy laws are vague but harsh. They require no proof of intent, only of "imputation, innuendo or insinuation, directly or indirectly."[26] In other words, blasphemy may be unwitting and in the eye of the beholder only. With malicious or angry clerics and other activists whipping up the crowds, the charge of blasphemy has triggered even more mob violence and vigilante justice than judicial proceedings, vile though the latter are.

Quite simply, blasphemy laws (and hate speech regulations in general) empower bullying and intimidation, and silence freedom. In countries such as Pakistan and Egypt, they even operate, as a former Pakistani Member of Parliament claims, as "slow motion religious cleansing," or as a "Salafi pogrom."[27] Does anyone wish to settle a score, muzzle a rival opinion, drive an enemy from the field? Accuse them of blasphemy (or hate) and the brutal machinery of oppression can take over and deal with them. Atrociously, Ghulam Ahmad Bilour, a Pakistani cabinet minister offered a $100,000 bounty for anyone killing the creator of the fourteen-minute video *Innocence of Muslims*, and volunteered to carry out the task himself. He even announced proudly that he was prepared to be hanged for doing it.[28]

There have been scores of controversial incidents where there was no actual violence, but the list of Muslim threats to artistic performances and academic presentations is appalling. So also are the honest arguments muzzled repeatedly by accusations of hate, bigotry and phobias of one kind or another. From Yale University to London's Tate Gallery, and from French rights activist Brigitte Bardot to novelist Michel Houellebecq, to Britain's Channel 4 canceling a screening of its documentary "Islam: The Untold Story" because of security threats, the lesson is surely clear.

It is time for the West to look in the mirror and face up to its own hypocrisies first, and then to turn back to be true to its heritage and to stand firmly for its view of rights. Civility should never be confused with cowardice, but to answer weakly is to court dismissal as a weakling. The heckler's veto has always been a menace to free speech, but how much more so the assassin's veto now.

It is also time for the West to say to Islam politely but firmly and in concert, "The way you defend your prophet demeans your faith. Your oppressive regimes, your popular rage, your mobs and your murderous mayhem do not strengthen your arguments or advance your cause. Your violent defenders are more damaging to Islam than a thousand insults. They are a reproach to the God you say you worship. You are responsible for how you live in your own countries and how you treat your own people, but this is our civilization, this is our way of life, and these are our freedoms. We prize freedom of conscience, we prize free speech, we prize debate, and you should know that when you are in our tent, this is the way we behave. We will not be silenced."

It is bad enough for the majority of Muslims in the world that the global image of their faith is now being shaped by Wahhabis, Salafis and extremists. But for those who prize freedom, the deeper problem is that Salman Rushdie now says that in the present climate of nervousness and fear, his novel *The Satanic Verses* could not be published today.[29] Free expression is being silenced in the name of avoiding blasphemy, heresy, insult and offense.

Even worse is the plain and awful fact is that in today's global climate, the Universal Declaration of Human Rights could not be passed—just as for different but equally shameful Western reasons, many issues that are crucial to the future of Western society will never be debated openly and freely as they need to be. The vigilante activists of hate speech, sometimes Muslim, sometimes homosexual, are lurking and ready to gang up on all who disagree with them.

Paul Marshall and Nina Shea summarize the menace well:

When politics and religion are intertwined, as they necessarily are in debates about blasphemy and insulting Islam, forbidding religious criticism means forbidding political criticism. Conversely, without religious debate there can be no political debate; without religious dissent there can be no political dissent. And without religious freedom, there can be no political freedom.[30]

Liberal attempts to counter hate speech have been notoriously unsatisfying. But the answer, need it be said, is to turn from fighting the negative with the negative to restoring and building the positive. Renew civic education, for example, and teach a virile understanding and practice of the three Rs of freedom of religion and belief (rights, responsibilities and respect). The robust civility that results will become a habit of the heart that drives incivility and hatred from the public square and restores a healthy discourse to free and open societies. Referring to the perennial danger of relying only on law at the expense of the habits of the heart, Rodney Smolla reminds us as a lawyer and constitutional expert himself, "In a just society, reason and tolerance must triumph over prejudice and hate. But that triumph is best achieved through education and not coercion."[31]

BEWARE LIBERALS BESTOWING EQUALITY

The second way in which liberals commonly become illiberal today is when they fight for equality in ways that undermine liberty. This danger runs like an undercurrent through many of the recent violations of liberty, and it requires far more discussion than it has been given. The lesson is unmistakable: *Those who become obsessed with the pursuit of equality through the principle of nondiscrimination, but at the expense of freedom, end by losing all three.*

This error has dogged the story of freedom down the ages, most infamously in the French Revolution. Named after the Attic innkeeper who was nicknamed "the racker," it is the politics of Procrustes that is becoming a serious danger again as same-sex equality orthodoxy is clashing with the equal rights of those who disagree with them—and with no conscience protection offered to the dissenters. The latter is important in issues such as the health care mandates because equality legislation without conscience protection can become a form of religious cleansing, wittingly or unwittingly: Violate your conscience or leave your profession. Or as some put it more bluntly, "Lump it or leave!"

Oxford University's bioethicist Julian Savulescu speaks for the zero-sum, scorched-earth mentality with astonishing candor: "If people are not prepared to offer legally permitted, efficient, and beneficial care to a patient because it conflicts with their values, they should not be doctors."[32] Mary Ann Glendon had warned earlier of just such logic on the other side of the Atlantic: "In its simple American form, the language of rights is the language of no compromise. The winner takes all and the loser has to get out of town."[33] But the brazen logic of such thinking still takes the breath away. With an unblushing arrogance, it is addressed openly to members of the faith that more than any other has shaped Western medicine and been the wellspring of our unique Western culture of giving and caring over the past two thousand years.

At one stroke, and with barely a decent moment of thought, let alone debate, such enthusiasts for enforced equality kill the goose that laid the golden egg. For who was it who built the hospitals and created an entire culture of caring for the sick, the poor and the dying? Yet doubtless these same people will still be surprised when the day dawns that they go out in the morning and find no golden eggs.

Once again, the convergence between Western illiberalism and non-Western authoritarianism is unmistakable. The perpetrators may be liberals and their intentions noble, but their actions in Western schools, hospitals and orphanages differ only in severity, not kind, from the ethnic cleansing by the Serbs in Kosovo and the religious cleansing by the radical imams in Pakistan.

There are three major kinds of equality—equality of condition, equality of opportunity and equality of outcome—and it is this third that is damaging, especially when it becomes doctrinaire and a matter almost of religious dogmatism. Unquestionably, there is often a contradiction and always a competition between liberty and equality. And when it comes to a needed balance between them, there are two pitfalls and two extremes to be avoided. On one side, many thinkers have gloried in inequality as the natural result of human differences and the natural expression of human striving for excellence. Nietzsche, for example, exalted the hero above the herd and considered equality, like pity and compassion, a tool by which the herd brought down the hero to its level of mediocrity. The trouble is that, left unchecked, such rank inequality easily grows to be an injustice that is only a few shades short of slavery. Or expressed in contemporary terms, the one-percenters in any field can become the revolting elites who disdain the ninety-nine-percenters of the masses below them.[34]

One the other side, the disciples of Procrustes have been conspicuous, especially in revolutionary periods. For example, Gracchus Babeuf declared brazenly in the French Revolution: "Society must be made to operate in such a way that it eradicates once for all the desires of a man to become richer, or wiser, or more powerful than others."[35]

Other thinkers have therefore recognized the importance of balancing liberty and equality. Both principles should be prized ideals in societies that aspire to be just as well as free and open. All humans should have the right to be free, just as all should be equally respected under the law, and all should have an equal opportunity to make the most of life. Freedom and equality are essential partners in the service of human flourishing, but they must be harnessed with care and the differences between the distinct forms of equality must be guarded constantly.

It is a shining mark of free and just societies that they strive for both ideals, but keeping the balance between them is the fly in the ointment. *For liberty often threatens equality, just as equality often threatens liberty, and too much inequality from too much liberty may threaten liberty just as much as too much equality without liberty does.* There is therefore a natural and persistent competition between the two ideals that requires the deft handling of a statesman—which is hardly the hallmark of today's crusaders for equality and nondiscrimination.

One side of the tension is plain. That liberty has downsides is obvious to all who take seriously the crooked timber of our human nature. There are many problems with the unbalanced and unsustainable views of freedom that are now current—for example, excessive individualism, the coarsening of society, the betrayal of the good life, the reinforcement of a culture of transgression and the creation of a moneyed elite. The plain fact is that modern Western liberty is undermining equality and fairness in many ways, and nowhere more than in the United States.

Yet for all its damaging consequences, we are still right to consider liberty good. At worst, freedom is double-edged. It not only fosters the dignity of difference and enhances the richness of diversity, but also serves to amplify our inequalities. Thus equality finds itself under challenge today from three directions:

- First, there is the obvious and insurmountable fact that according to most measures—strength, speed, intelligence, talent and wealth, for example—all humans are simply not equal and never will be. From our first brush with schooling and examinations to the heights of Olympic sports, to businesses of all kinds, and the story of men in war, the glory of contest and competition stands as a constant reminder of our human inequalities that no ruler, no law and no zeal can ever eradicate. To confuse equality and identity, and therefore enforce conformity, is silly as well as wrong.

• Second, the inequalities produced by liberty today have become so severe and the contemporary foundations for the belief in human equality so flimsy, now that the traditional Jewish and Christian foundations have been dismantled, that those who affirm the ideal of equality do so over a yawning abyss. Left to nature—without human intervention, that is—humans are obviously unequal. And without God to anchor their equality as his children, the rights to liberty and equality have been made into *fiat* rights, mere paper promises and arbitrary conventions. In the words of the atheist philosopher A. C. Grayling, they are nothing more than "the result of [human] *decisions* to regard them as such."[36] Such equality is essentially artificial and flimsy.

• Third, from the French to the Russian and the Chinese revolutions, history repeats monotonously that humans can only be made fully and formally equal by the most draconian measures that result in silencing dissent, flouting diversity and flattening out distinctions. Liberty by definition is uncoerced, whereas equality is artificial and can be established only by coercion.

But that is only one side of the problem. What of the other? How does equality threaten freedom? Justice, with her eyes blindfolded, is the universal symbol that all human beings deserve equal respect under law. True justice is no respecter of persons. Her scales are balanced. But equal respect under law is one thing and many formal notions of equality and a passion for doctrinaire egalitarianism are another.

There are three dangerous tendencies that rear their head in history's recurring drives for equality and nondiscrimination. They are not always writ large and crude, as in the grand revolutionary drives on behalf of French *égalité* or the classless society of communism. They may be writ small and with more a more sophisticated hand, as in liberal drives for nondiscrimination now. But for those who would defend the liberal society, the damaging tendencies need watching. As Oxford's Roger Trigg warns, "Any state's attempt to control religion, in the name of equality, can challenge the very freedom on which democracy rests."[37]

- First, when the pursuit of equality is elevated to being the ultimate good, rather than one ideal among others, it is likely to be driven by envy, jealousy and resentment until it grows into a passion for formal equality or equality-as-uniformity. If this happens, it will grow in turn into a zero-sum game in which competitors brook no rivals, scorn any negotiation of rights and obliterate all claims to rights that stand in their way.

  Today, this lethal brand of egalitarianism, crusading under the banner of nondiscrimination, is often fueled by a passion for moral purity that allows no other moral criteria apart from equality and therefore becomes as zealous for its ruthless consistency as Torquemada was for his orthodoxy. "*Égalité*," Tocqueville wrote, "is an expression of envy. It means, in the real heart of every republican, 'No one shall be better off that I am.'"[38]

- Second, the pursuit of equality and nondiscrimination has a broad flattening effect, because it confuses equality of personhood with equality of behavior and therefore opens the door to amorality. On the one hand, it irons out diversity by reducing individuality to social categories labeled according to gender, class and race. On the other hand, it rules out all moral and social criteria and considerations other than equality, and therefore encourages the equal rights of all behaviors regardless of moral criteria or social consequences.

Thus in a liberal society prizing radical equality, behaviors that were once considered wrong now become one more practice in the mosaic of diverse practices that can each demand equal rights with all others. If, for example, equality alone is the criterion, on what grounds should anyone withhold equal rights from the advocates of polyamory, polygamy, child marriage, female genital circumcision, pedophilia, incest and sex with animals? And how will anyone voting against such practices be able to escape the automatic accusation of prejudice, bigotry and hatred?

As stressed earlier, freedom of thought, conscience, religion and belief protects believers and not beliefs, and the distinction is vital. It is a similar mistake here to confuse the equal protection of believers with the equal protection of behaviors. Were this trend to go further, the liberal state would not survive the dire relativism and the sloppy indifference to right and wrong, prudence and folly that would result. In the end, it would be impossible for such a state to ground the foundations of its own liberalism.

• Third, the pursuit of equality and nondiscrimination requires a strong umpire to adjudicate the claims of the "disadvantaged" and the "victims," and then impose the socially engineered solutions in their favor. This becomes more urgent all the time because an equality-based society produces ever more claimants to be the aggrieved and victimized on the grounds that they are not treated equally. Thus an engineered equality means an enforced equality, which in turn means an enforcer. Such equality always increases lack of trust between groups and reinforces rivalry, insecurities, jealousy and paranoia.

The result carries an almost mathematical certainty: The drive to achieve a more formally equal society ends by more and more legal interventions, a steady erosion of individual liberty and personal responsibility, and the relentless strengthening of the central deciding authority. Society may be made more equal, but individuals will become less free, and the umpiring state (or university) will become stronger and more intrusive. Call the umpires experts or specialists or administrators, but the result is a new form of Plato's Guardians, the elite and unequal egalitarians who lop off the limbs of all who do not fit the beds in their inn. As Woody Allen quipped, "I believe there is something out there watching over us. Unfortunately, it's the government."

In short, it is true that inequality is the price of diversity with liberty. But it is also true that the removal of all inequalities kills off liberty and stifles diversity with a blanketing uniformity. We should all be equal before the law, and equal in our opportunities. But we should never be forced to become the same as each other, and equality need not mean uniform treatment, especially of behaviors. Those who confuse these notions grease the slipway for an authoritarian state and an illiberal university before which no rights are inalienable and no conscience is inviolable.

Reviewing the Napoleonic aftermath of the French Revolution, Benjamin de Constant wrote in 1815, "It is quite remarkable that uniformity never met with more favour than in a revolution raised in the name of the rights and the liberty of men."[39] As in so many contemporary debates, the fundamental question arises, what kind of a society do we wish to be? What kind of a world do we wish to build and live in? And in this case, what sort of a society are we creating when the *free exercise* of religion and belief is reduced to the mere freedom to opt out?

Are all doctors who disagree morally with abortion or assisted suicide going to be required to obey the law or give up medicine? Will teachers who object to homosexual practice be required to affirm and celebrate it as a matter of justice in their classrooms or retire from teaching? Will universities refuse recognition to religious groups who refuse to abandon religious criteria in their selection of their own leaders? Will laws be passed requiring employers to provide free abortions for their employees? Will Western governments refuse to provide grants to international religious NGOs that refuse to favor the agenda of the new sexual orthodoxy in the developing world? Will parents lose their rights to shape their children's values over against the state's values, as Richard Dawkins and others have proposed?

The mind boggles that such possibilities have all been raised in the lands that pioneered freedom of thought, conscience, religion and belief. But whenever there is a clash of rights today, it is routinely said that freedom of religion and belief should be the right that must give way, and that no conscience exemptions are to be granted. Yet those are only a few of the demands and proposals that have been put forward recently by the zealots for equality and nondiscrimination. Once again, questions have to be asked: Who are the true liberals and free thinkers now? By what right are the equalizers equalizing? And who will equalize the equalizers, when history shows that they will equalize everybody but themselves? What will become of the status of freedom of religion and belief if conscience clauses are routinely denied in the general rush to press for equality and nondiscrimination? Ironically, the English-speaking countries have an unparalleled tradition of recognizing the rights of freedom of conscience, for example, over war, medical treatment and the like. But now they are growing niggardly in granting that right to the very faith that made the principle possible in the first place.

Christians, Jews, Mormons and Muslims are only a few of the

major religious groups that find themselves at odds with aspects of the sexual revolution of the last fifty years. It is entirely appropriate for their followers to be challenged to live according to a higher and different standard within a society that they believe has chosen different or lower standards. But it is quite another for them to be expelled from professions and careers for profound moral disagreements over these standards. Indeed, in the case of the Muslims, such misguided egalitarianism will only reinforce the trend for them to play the multicultural card and press for alternative courts so that they can be a law unto themselves—thus shattering the bonds of equality even further.

Liberals with their busy impatience for progress and the future often lack a sense of history and a feel for irony. The eminent English historian Thomas Babington Macaulay, a Whig as well as a historian, wrote to an American friend in 1857: "I have long been convinced that institutions purely democratic must, sooner or later, destroy liberty, or civilization, or both. . . . You may think that your country enjoys an exemption from these evils. I frankly own to you that I am of a very different opinion. Your fate, I believe, is certain."[40] There is of course a better way than the zero-sum power plays of the equality purists. Such a way would require at least the following components:

- First, a humility to recognize the ironies produced by the pursuit of equality—including the fact that real equality requires differential treatment. Just and free equality is not achieved by a formal flattening of differences but by recognizing genuine diversity and treating different communities differently because of the distinction between belief and behavior.

- Second, a commitment to negotiate rights, whenever there is a clash of rights, so that no right is allowed to obliterate other rights and reduce all rights to the level of a mere power game.

- Third, a determination to avoid the domination of one right over other rights, and therefore to apply the principle of forbearance and seek for a reasonable accommodation on a case-by-case basis.

No one pressing for formal equality and absolute nondiscrimination should fool themselves. The alternative to a negotiated approach is to keep on with the culture warring of the conservative activists or the scorched-earth tactics of the liberal activists, and to hasten the end of justice and freedom for all. Conscience protection has become a prime concern in the Western world, and the balance of liberty and equality is a task for the cool hands of the prudent rather than the hot heads of the zealous.

TIME TO RETHINK

It is clearly time for both conservatives and liberals to examine and reassess their approaches, and to acknowledge where their well-intentioned efforts have been damaging to freedom and counterproductive to their own causes too.

On one side, liberals must remember that though speech is vital for free and open societies, it is best reformed and helped to flourish by teaching and demonstrating positive principles and attitudes. For example, use stories and examples as well as principles to teach the three Rs of freedom of thought and conscience, and they will become habits of the heart. As such, they will be far more powerful than negative concepts such as sensitivity and hate alone.

The recent liberal resort to sensitivity training, hate and phobia, and to negative tactics in general, is understandable as a frustrated response to the lack of progress and the deepening bitterness in the culture wars. But it has now become part of the problem and not the solution. And again, there is an ominous warning to free societies in danger of forgetting what their hard-won freedoms entail.

If we are not clear and positive about *our ways* of practicing freedom of thought and conscience, which have been won on behalf of all humanity, we will have no grounds for resisting *their ways* that will prove disastrous for the human future as a whole.

On the other side, conservatives must rethink the *whatever it takes* attitudes of their culture warring over the past fifty years. What they have taken to be courage has often been foolish and counterproductive too. The lessons of the last decades of high-profile religious and conservative activism are incontrovertible, though ironic:

- First, religious conservatives have themselves become politicized, and in their growing trust in politics to do what politics can never do, they have mirrored a fatal flaw of left-wing politics since the 1920s. As Richard John Neuhaus intoned so often, "The first thing to say about politics is that politics is not the first thing." Politics is downstream from many of the real sources of the problems, so—to switch metaphors—it is forever closing the barn door after the horse has bolted. And as always, mixing religion and politics badly is a sure recipe for producing more bad politics and bad religion.

- Second, in their pursuit of a politics that is purely partisan, conservative and often angrily defensive, they have produced the opposite of what they set out to achieve. Seeking to advance the role of religion in public life, they have massively increased the number of those opposed to it being in public life and disastrously solidified the "God gap" between religious conservatives and secular liberals.

- Third and most ironically of all, religiously based conservative activists have created such a backlash against politicized religion that they have turned away an unprecedented number of people, including the younger generation, from faith itself. In America's case this massive defection is both historic and fateful.

In short, starting from a legitimate concern that religion was being pushed out of public life, these well-intentioned conservatives have not only failed in their purpose but succeeded in pushing growing numbers of people away not only from public life but from faith too.[41]

Will responsible religious believers come to recognize the irreligious results of their fellow believers? Will thoughtful conservatives have the courage to examine the unconservative consequences of their actions? Will European religious conservatives learn from the follies of their well-meaning American counterparts? Will self-critical liberals have the honesty to examine the unintended illiberalism of some of their recent positions? Are the secular tone deaf about to admit their impairment and show their need for help? Will true freedom of thought and conscience advance once more and get the better of today's secularist prejudice, just as it overcame religious intolerance earlier? In the bitter and fractious mood of the culture wars, with secularist voices as loud and lucrative as religious voices, no one should hold their breath.

At the very least, what matters is the frank acknowledgment that a genuine understanding of a vital global issue is still being choked off by tone deafness, just as urgently needed practical solutions are being held back by mistaken approaches that are well-meaning but counterproductive. Too many are simply looking for answers in the wrong place. But it is time to turn now to the positive itself.

Again, it is time, and past time, to ponder the question. What does it say of us and our times that the Universal Declaration of Human Rights could not be passed today? And what does it say of the future of freedom of thought, conscience, religion and belief if it can be neglected and threatened even in the United States, where it once developed most fully—that it can be endangered anywhere? Who will step forward now to champion the cause of freedom for the good of all and for the future of humanity?

8

A CIVIL AND COSMOPOLITAN
PUBLIC SQUARE

THE SEVENTH STEP IN THE REVALUATION *is to explore the vision of a civil public square that provides the greatest realization for the greatest number of people of a genuine soul freedom for people of all faiths and none, and offers the surest road to civility and stability in the global public square.*

At the present moment we are seeing violent conflicts at the extremes and various levels of culture warring at the heart of many societies—including the United States. The world is torn between varieties of the sacred public square and the naked public square, between the polar extremes of Iran and China, between the styles of the religious right and the secular left. Neither extreme, as I have argued, does justice to the equality and universality of freedom of thought and conscience for all citizens and all human beings, let alone the challenges of a world in which "everyone is everywhere."

But what is the alternative, the vision and model of a civil public square that is essential to establishing soul freedom? A civil public square is a vision of public life in which citizens of all faiths and none are free to enter and engage public life on the basis of their faith, as a matter of freedom of thought, conscience and free exercise, but within an agreed framework of what is understood and respected to be just and free for people of all other faiths too, and thus for the common good.

This framework is political and not religious. In John Courtney Murray's apt description, it is a matter of "articles of peace" rather than "articles of faith."[1] As such, it has to be agreed, affirmed and then handed down from generation to generation until it truly becomes a habit of the heart for the citizenry. At its core are the three Rs of freedom of thought and conscience: rights, responsibilities and respect. As mentioned earlier, a right for one person is a right for another, and a responsibility for both and for everyone. Freedom of thought and conscience means that there are no special rights, no favored faiths and no protected beliefs. It is the consciences of believers, not the content of beliefs, that are protected.

Reciprocity, mutuality and universality are the key principles of this vision of a civil public square. In this sense a civil public square is the political embodiment of the Golden Rule. "Treat others with the respect you would like to be treated with yourself, and protect for others the rights you would like protected for yourself." Thus a right for a Christian is automatically a right for a Jew, an atheist, a Muslim, a Buddhist, a Mormon, a Hindu, a Scientologist and for every believer in every faith under the sun as the earth turns. All human rights are the rights of all human beings. They are for the good of all.

Such talk is apt to sound like hot air and to produce a smirk from the cynics, and with good reason. Many people today have become too cynical, and many of our countries have become too cantankerous to be able to afford another passing spasm of civility talk.

There are in fact solid reasons why civility is scorned today. First, civility is confused with niceness and dismissed as a wimp word. At best it is viewed only as a matter of manners and etiquette, having a mild tone of voice or feeling a refined distaste for the nastiness of differences. Far from it. Civility is a tough-minded classical virtue and duty that enables citizens to take their public differences seriously, debate them robustly, and negotiate and decide them peacefully rather than violently.

Second, civility is too often discussed by itself and taken as a stand-alone virtue, as if it could somehow magically transform public life into sweetness and light all by itself. Again, far from it. Civility is a classical virtue and duty, essential for both republics and democracies and especially for societies that need to negotiate a strong degree of diversity among their citizens. But civility is not an end in itself. It stands in the service of the higher good—soul freedom for all. Indeed, the greatest benefit of civility is that it provides the best conditions within which freedom of thought and conscience can grow strong and active.

As such, civility is only one part of the complete arsenal of well-formed citizens, who together can take pride and responsibility in building and maintaining a healthy civil society and a vigorous but civil public square. Just as an untended garden will run to weeds, so an uneducated citizenry will be quickly be overrun by power-mongers, manipulators, cynics and moneyed seducers. That will always happen when the better angels of our nature have been neglected. What such people are destroying is not just civility but soul freedom itself, as well as the health of the society, the bonding of the commonwealth and the duties of their own citizenship. Hand in hand with the complete responsibilities of citizenship, civility makes for a thriving republic and a truly open democracy. It speaks, after all, to our human nature as men and women who can speak, listen, weigh and decide, and live up to our human responsibility.

FROM SWORD TO WORD

Needless to say, such a vision of a civil public square has numerous implications. For a start, a civil public square is absolutely essential to free and open societies, for without it there is no healthy public life, and there can be no open ground for discussing the common good in terms illuminated by public reason. As Cicero argued passionately before the Roman senate, if public reasoning together is undermined, so also is the very foundation of what constitutes a republic. All who care for free societies must therefore review their assumptions and follow the logic of these assumptions in rebuilding and maintaining the public square with care—whatever the costs of facing down the obdurate religious extremists on one side and the obdurate secularist extremists on the other.

Civility in public life carries many positive consequences, but there are also some notable traps into which it is easy to fall. The right to free exercise in public life requires civility, and civility in public life assumes in turn that public discourse must shift from coercion to persuasion—from the "sword" to the "word" as Roger Williams put it.[2] Those who would prevail in public affairs have to persuade others in the public square. To make a persuasive public case under the conditions of contemporary pluralism means that advocates of any policy have to translate their case into terms that make sense to others. They have to know how to address the interests and ideals of others and persuade believers of very different faiths and worldviews.

Beware a hidden trap at this point. Many people today fear that someone's "right to enter and engage public life" is tantamount to a license to "impose their views on everyone else." Needless to say, nothing in a postmodern world is held to be worse than imposing morals on anyone else (as if all law were not a moral imposition of some sort), so the obvious response to this fear is to deny free exercise in public life. But this is doubly undemocratic.

First, it curbs the democratic freedom of free exercise, and second, it forgets that in a democracy no one can impose their views on others without persuading others that their views are right and good, and then winning a sufficient majority to enact a law in their favor. Whether the prevailing majority is liberal and hopes to promote same-sex marriage, or conservative and seeks to deny it, it can only prevail (impose) through democratic persuasion, and even then there are always the rights that protect the minority.

This commitment to persuasion is vital and quite different from the *fiat* rulings of judges. The "freedom to enter and engage" entails in turn both a freedom and a duty to persuade, and this requirement holds good for conservatives and liberals alike. Such persuasion in its turn requires publicly accessible arguments, which is one of several reasons why we are now said to be in the great age of apologetics. From the millions presenting their "Daily Me" on Facebook to the grand political speeches jousting in national elections, never have so many so often been in the business of presenting themselves, explaining themselves and defending themselves to others.

Watch out for another trap at this point. Contrary to recent demands and much misunderstanding, persuasion and its need for publicly accessible arguments does not mean that public discourse has to have a secular haircut and be shorn of all religious content when entering the public square. What it really means is this: We need to recognize that arguing with people who do not understand us is ineffective, and citing authorities to those who do not share them is a waste of time. But the reason why we must all translate in order to persuade is not because of any phony threat that we are violating the separation of church and state, but because of our desire to persuade people of different positions; different perspectives and different policies. Persuasion, in short, is not imposition. It is a highly liberal exercise, and it follows naturally from freedom of thought and conscience and free exercise.

DIFFERENCES MAKE A DIFFERENCE

Like civility itself, the vision of a civil public square is surrounded by a thicket of misunderstandings and misgivings. Three are especially damaging.

One common misunderstanding is that a civil public square must be reached by a search for a lowest common denominator unity, whether a "no label" political movement or a form of interfaith dialogue and interfaith cooperation. No-label movements are well-intentioned and understandable reactions to the gridlock of extreme partisanship. But they are utterly misguided because politics is essentially partisan, and civility stands for a protection and negotiation of differences, not their elimination.

Interfaith dialogue has more to say for it than the no-label movement, and there are many examples of such initiatives today, including "A Common Word" initiative launched by Islamic religious leaders, Prince Ghazi of Jordan's "Amman Message," Karen Armstrong's "Charter of Compassion," former Prime Minister Tony Blair's Faith Foundation and many others.

Such interfaith efforts are welcome and mostly beneficial, as are the many new initiatives in citizen diplomacy. As Winston Churchill said, it is always better to "jaw jaw" than to "war war." But it also has to be said frankly that these initiatives are limited, and they will never reach the desired goal we are seeking. At the end of the day, whatever reconciliation is effected by interfaith dialogue is limited to some religions rather than all, and the reconciliation usually does not include citizens who are secularists. Besides, the blunt fact is the differences between core beliefs, including secularism, are irreducible and ultimate. As such, they will never be bridged by any lowest common denominator, however long we talk and however nice we are.

Besides, contrary to the foggy multiculturalism of the postmodern era, it is important to go beyond a celebration of diversity in the abstract. This often turns out to be one group's way of promoting its difference over others. What we need is to examine what those differences really are in reality. Differences make a difference, both to individuals and to whole societies and even civilizations. Those differences are important, and they have to be engaged honestly and debated fearlessly.

So once again, let there be no misunderstanding: a civil public square does not require or depend on interfaith dialogue. Nor does it require any ultimate ecumenical unity. That hope, which is attractive to some and faithless to others, is utopian. Rather, a civil public square is forged through an agreed political framework of rights, responsibilities and respect, within which each faith is free to be faithful to its own beliefs and yet responsible to know how to deal respectfully and civilly with the vital differences of other beliefs.

Here lies one of the greatest advantages of the civil public square: *it protects the freedom to be faithful.* A civil public square promotes the highest freedom of thought and conscience, the strongest civility between faiths and the greatest freedom for each faith to be true to its own truth claims. Under no other model—neither the naked public square nor the sacred public square—are all citizens encouraged to be true to the faiths by which they live and yet taught to be civil to others and care for the common good of the society in which they live.

WINNERS AND LOSERS

The false allure of dialogue as the solution to diversity dies hard. But consider a better picture and precedent for the civil public square: the impact of the Queensberry rules on the sport of boxing. Romans are often accused of hypocrisy because they banned boxing while still loving their gladiatorial games. Without a doubt, boxing was once brutal, with bare-knuckle fights that often ended in the death of one or other fighter. But boxing was transformed into a modern sport in the nineteenth century when one of England's sporting aristocrats, the Marquess of Queensberry, lent his name to new rules. Boxing was put into a ring and under both rules and a referee. But it was still a competition, and there were still winners and losers. Boxers may momentarily touch gloves at the start of a fight, and if they do not want to be disqualified, they do not punch below the belt. But they go all out to win, on points or by a knockout.

In the same way, civility is not a matter of being inoffensive, of squeamishness about differences, a form of politically correct sensitivity training or a requirement that people are unable to be true to what they believe. Civility serves the interests of both truth and wisdom by providing the setting for the tough-minded exchange of views that is necessary for the best and wisest policies to prevail, and yet still makes possible a peaceable community. It is thus a republican virtue as well as a democratic necessity (with a small *r* and a small *d*).

There are important differences between the faiths and between their worldviews and policies. Debating the differences between the faiths themselves is usually best left out of the public square, for the latter is the arena for debating issues of our common life. But the differences between the policies that grow out of different faiths are proper subject matter of the public square. They are in fact the differences that make a difference and are vital to considering what kind of societies we wish to be. These differences therefore need to be debated, and robust, tough-minded debates about issues that matter will and should always end with winners and losers. One side will prevail through persuasion, while the other will lose, at least for the time being—and if possible, the loser will ready itself for a better campaign and a more successful outcome the next time. Needless to say, all I am describing is the natural course of democracy.

In short, many of today's government "consultations" are a sham and a fig leaf to provide cover for some administrative fiat of one kind or another. But civility and contest are real, robust and not opposites. Civility serves and supports competition and contest, while ensuring that they in turn do not tear apart the common good but build the commonwealth.

THE RIGHT TO BE WRONG

Another widespread misunderstanding is that civility is a form of sloppy tolerance that is the virtue of those who believe little or nothing—in a word, indifferentism, symbolized by a Frenchman's shrug of the shoulders or a teenager's "Whatever." Curiously, this fear is found today not only among religious fundamentalists but also among atheist fundamentalists, as in the earlier example of Dawkins's shameless intolerance.

Behind this fear lies a long and still-running history, for those who prize truth and correct thinking of any kind are prone to defend their orthodoxy in ways that are intolerant of dissent. They therefore think it right to punish deviance and heresy in the name of truth, and to discriminate against those who disagree with their orthodoxy or deviate from their majority opinion. In one form or another, history has witnessed too much of the dangerous mentality that "error has no rights." Over the years this procrustean bent of orthodoxy has morphed from Roman magistrates to Roman Catholic inquisitors, to Soviet commissars, to apostasy-hunting Muslim ayatollahs, to "faith heads" attacking new atheists, to well-meaning equality-seeking university administrators. Today, it not only strides beneath the sound of the minaret but stalks the halls of the academy.

Once again, Roger Williams was among the tiny band that first established genuine toleration and in a truly thoroughgoing way. Before then, moves in that direction had been intermittent and inconsistent. Even such men as Locke and Milton, now famous as advocates of toleration, actually restricted their toleration in their time. Earlier still, in the sixteenth century, Sir Thomas More reached out toward toleration in his classic imaginary work *Utopia* ("no one should suffer for their religion"), often cited by his admirers today. But when the Lord Chancellor came to the real affairs of state, he believed that executing heretics was necessary for the state and beneficial for the offenders—and he backed his theory with determined action and personally made heretics "suffer for their religion."

Draconian examples are rarer in our own time, though still harshly alive in the communist and Muslim worlds. In countries such as Iran and Pakistan, charges of apostasy are still a nearly automatic death sentence, and courageous leaders who stand against such injustice have paid with their lives.

In the Western world both the fear and the response are milder. But at its heart is a simple fallacy: that respecting a person's right to believe means accepting the results of what he or she believes, so that toleration automatically slides into indifference to truth and permissiveness toward morality—and with such a notion of civility it is bound to.

Not at all. Consider the following sentence: *"The right to believe anything" does not mean that "anything anyone believes is right."* The first half of the sentence is a matter of freedom of conscience, whereas the second is dangerous nonsense. People have every right to believe what they believe, based on freedom of thought and conscience, and others must respect that right. But what they believe may have consequences that are muddle-headed, socially disastrous, morally wrong or even profoundly evil. Others then have a responsibility as well as a right to differ with them—robustly, but always civilly and persuasively. After all, we are all responsible to raise the question of what kind of a people we want to be, and what kind of a society we wish to live in.

Once again, freedom of thought, conscience, religion and belief protects believers and not beliefs. Animists have the absolute right to believe in animism, but free societies are free to challenge and outlaw practices such genital mutilation, let alone human sacrifice. Muslims have the absolute right to believe in Islam and surrender to Allah, but free democracies are free to challenge and outlaw such notions as defamation and apostasy that are so destructive of free speech, let alone honor killings and suicide martyrdoms. More controversially, Western conservatives and Western liberals have the right to believe what they each believe and disbelieve what they each disbelieve, but Western societies are free to challenge and outlaw the policies of one or the other so that society either favors or forbids such contested practices as abortion and same-sex marriage.

Behind that simple point about the limits of tolerance and respect is an elementary truth: the recognition that our minds are finite and that to err is human, so the free-thinking person must always be open to the challenge of new ideas. Our right to be wrong is therefore a requirement of freedom and an essential for growth. Without that right, we could never grow in understanding, be freed from error or learn through discovery. And we could never escape from people who are arrogant and the tyrannical, who never admit they are wrong and who punish us for our differences from them.

Away then with the high and mighty presumption that claims its right to force its views on others. Away with all heavy-handed attempts to curb freedom of thought and conscience from the outside. An end to any and all authorities that would tyrannize the mind by external means—whether grand inquisitors, czars, ayatollahs, politically correct university administrations, well-meaning sanitizers of our speech, activist vigilantes or anyone who would stand between each of us and our consciences.

DANGEROUSLY UNSTABLE?

The last widespread misgiving about civility and a civil public square is that, at best, the two ideas are inherently and dangerously unstable, and therefore exceedingly foolish in today's world. In protecting the equal rights of all beliefs, they are surely opening the door to beliefs that will undermine the system itself. A common current fear, for example, is that Muslim extremists may use the freedom of the civil public square to press for their own advantage in order to gain the victory and put the "enemies of God" out of the game—"one man, one vote, one time," as the Middle Eastern maxim goes—or more simply, to exploit the freedom of the host countries in order to plot their destruction.

That scenario is certainly a possibility and a serious danger. All free and open societies are inherently unstable, and in fact there are two major ways, and not just one, in which an open society can always be undermined. The obvious danger is that, in their freedom, free societies may open the door to the enemies of freedom. The other is that freedom may breed such tolerance that it degenerates into anything-goes indifference, to the point where the whole system slumps into apathy. It was in fact a combination of these two follies, reinforced by an ill-considered multiculturalism, that led the British and the Dutch to welcome Muslim extremists and allow them to build their enclaves with such destructive consequences.

But neither of these potential dangers is unique to the vision of a civil public square. They are inherent in the very notion of democracy itself. They can be countered only by a vigilant attention to the obvious requirements of a healthy, open society—including the vital importance of civic education and commitment to free, unfettered debate that engages with any and all ideas that are inimical to its health. Does any freedom-loving society deserve to survive if its citizens pay so little attention to freedom that they allow hostility or indifference to prevail through their own carelessness?

The Egypt of the Pharaohs certainly lasted longer than the democracy of Pericles and Demosthenes, but that is not an argument for giving up on democracy. It means, rather, that if we value democracy, we attend to the essentials that are necessary if free and open societies are to flourish and endure.

Some may fear that this rich, full notion of soul freedom for all is a mirage, or that this vision of civility and a civil public square is an impossible pipe dream. Such misgivings must be investigated thoroughly and answered if we are to progress. "Every truth passes through three stages before it is recognized," Arthur Schopenhauer wrote. "In the first, it is ridiculed, in the second it is opposed, in the third it is regarded as self-evident." Only time can show how realistic freedom is for humanity, but our convictions and decisions today are what will shape the outcome of those questions tomorrow.

Again, it is time, and past time, to ponder the question. What does it say of us and our times that the Universal Declaration of Human Rights could not be passed today? And what does it say of the future of freedom of thought, conscience, religion and belief if it can be neglected and threatened even in the United States, where it once developed most fully—that it can be endangered anywhere? Who will step forward now to champion the cause of freedom for the good of all and for the future of humanity?

9

LATER THAN WE THINK

THE EIGHTH STEP IN THE REVALUATION is *to forge a partnership between responsible religious and secularist leaders in order to take action now on the practical requirements for a constructive way forward for humankind, beginning with a declaration of the fundamental principles of the freedom of thought and conscience—soul freedom for all peoples and all nations. But it should be understood clearly that the moment of opportunity to achieve this task is closing and will not last long.*

The story is told of the "good soldier" who saw soldiers firing from their trenches at other soldiers in the opposing trenches. Leaping up, he ran out into the no-man's land between them, waving his arms and shouting at the top of his voice, "Stop! Stop shooting! There are people on the other side!"

Needless to say, the good soldier was an idiot—well meaning, perhaps, but an idiot who simply didn't understand the spoken and unspoken conditions of war that to most of his fellows needed no spelling out. To some people, this book's proposal may appear as naive and foolish as that. Humans fight. We always will fight. We have fought with fists, with clubs, with swords and now we fight with AK-47s, with drones, nuclear warheads and computers. We have always found battlefields on the land, the sea and the air, as regular soldiers or as guerillas, terrorists and vigilantes, so why wouldn't we turn op-ed pages, blogs and public squares into battlegrounds too? Surely the "better angels of our nature" are the stuff of dreams, and not worthy of anyone living within a century of Auschwitz and Hiroshima. Or so it is commonly said.

Such cynicism will always find it easy to recruit subscribers today, as will the coward's path to appeasement. There is a Middle Eastern maxim that "Extremists go all the way, while moderates just go away." But that of course would leave the field free for extremism. And both cynicism and cowardice are countered by the long, costly struggle on behalf of freedom and justice by thousands of people who know well what the world would be like if the horrors of the past were magnified in the future on an overcrowded and interconnected planet.

I, for one, stand with all who refuse to give up so weakly. We are the heirs of the many centuries of determined if never fully successful experiments in freedom and justice, and we would be careless beyond all excuse if we were to turn our backs on both the past and the future, and squander such a heritage in the present generation.

That extreme folly is not the end of the challenge we now face. In the opening words of this work I said that one of the world's great imperatives is to discover whether we humans have a solid enough reason to believe in the human dignity and worth of every last one of us. The point is far from rhetorical. Western civilization at its best, with its clearly Jewish and Christian roots, has championed the highest view of universal human dignity the world has ever known. Unquestionably, it has also contradicted that view in practice far too often. But it is such a view of human worth that lies behind the best of the reform movements in the West, including the abolition of slavery, as well as the recognition and expansion of human rights and civil rights in the last century.

That entire accomplishment is now in question, as views have arisen that undermine such a view of human dignity, and degrade the worth of individual humans in disastrous ways. Chief among the menaces are three that pose the greatest danger:

- First are the many forms of *reductionism*, when certain styles of thinking reduce other human beings in significant ways, such as reducing us to nothing but our genes, our mechanistic capacities, our animal status or our social and occupational functions, or simply treating us as statistics. In each case, what Martin Buber called the I-Thou relationship that is proper and vital between humans is lowered to I-It, and there is nothing inalienable and inviolable left. After all, real-life humans work, dream, bear children, get angry and feel hurts and disappointment, but "statistics don't bleed."

- Second are the different kinds of *determinism*, the modern views that have followed Spinoza's insistence that because humans are caught in the world of physical necessity, notions such as freedom and responsibility are merely useful fictions and we are really only determined—whether economically in Karl Marx's view, biologically in Charles Darwin's, psychologically in Sigmund Freud's, chemically in Jacques Monod's or genetically in the view of the sociobiologists. "Free will is an illusion," writes atheist philosopher Sam Harris typically. "Our wills are simply not of our own making."[1]

- Third are the varieties of *collectivism* that have no final place for the individual, but see each one of us as outweighed and overshadowed by the interests and imperatives of the collective, such as the general will, the state, the party, and the will of history.

Needless to say, the history of the last century and a half has already underscored heavily that such bad ideas have baleful consequences, and that the gap between the lightning and the thunder is shortening all the time as the storm approaches the heart of the Western world. So no one should view the current assaults on human dignity as anything other than consequential and certainly not a matter of theory only. As we lift our eyes to the horizons of our world, the time is later than we think, and the options before us are fewer than we realize.

What has helped to cement the supreme worth of every last person on earth in international law is the notion of crimes against humanity. This term came from a Russian proposal in 1915 in response to the horror of the Turkish massacre of the Armenians. It replaced the more limited terms of the wording of a draft that referred only to crimes "against Christianity and civilization." The notion was therefore the silver lining in the first genocidal slaughter of the twentieth century. But powerful though the term is, it is also question begging. What is it about humanity and the worth of each human person that makes a crime against humanity so vile and egregious?

Today's answers have become stunningly unclear. Professor Peter Singer of Princeton University, for example, views human uniqueness as "speciesism," so he argues that we have no more inherent rights than animals. He then sets out the result with astonishing candor: "There is no reason to think that a fish suffers less when dying in a net than a fetus suffers during an abortion, [hence] the argument for not eating fish is much stronger than the argument against abortion."[2] Or as he states even more baldly, "The life of a new-born baby is of less value to it than the life of a pig, a dog, or a chimpanzee is to the nonhuman animal."[3]

Will Singer and others like him live to rue the day when their ideas are commonplace and another round of victims bears the brunt of their consequences? Do such activists really believe they are raising animals to the level of humans, and that they will not lower humans to the level of animals? Can anyone doubt that such ideas will not again produce their own dark harvest of human degradation? And who this time will stand against the degraders as the Allies stood against the Nazis, when the Allies themselves are tomorrow's degraders and the spokesmen are their elites at the supposed pinnacle of their culture? "Never again," we have intoned solemnly ever since the end of World War II, but who would have believed how and where the "all over again" would have come from this time around?

No one should be under any illusions about the peril of the spiritual and moral confusions at the heart of our culture, and especially about the lack of rationally justified foundations for human dignity, liberty and equality. The foundations for the humanity of our culture is perilously unstable and close to collapse, and it is entirely possible that another round of the thought experiments and human engineering of Heinrich Himmler and Josef Mengele are on their way—and under the aegis of the best and brightest of yet another country that prides itself on the sophisticated culture and progressive thinking of its post-Christian freedom.

In short, the present proposal for soul freedom for all is far from naive. It is something of the nature of a last chance. And it is fired not only by hope but by an open-eyed realism about what might happen if soul freedom for all continues to be ignored as it is now.

THE POINT IS TO CHANGE IT

There is still another aspect of the challenge. Even if the world succeeds in maintaining solid grounds for human dignity, the practical task remains: making soul freedom, civility and a civil public square into living political realities. In other words, moving beyond talk.

"Philosophers have only interpreted the world in various ways; the point is to change it." Nowhere is Marx's famous saying more appropriate than over the problem we are examining. Freedom of thought, conscience, religion and belief must be established for all, and the global challenge of living with our deepest differences must be solved. Yet topics such as freedom of conscience, civility, culture warring, religious extremism, religiously based violence and a host of attendant issues have all been studied to death. Millions of dollars, oceans of ink, thousands of pages and hundreds of lawsuits have been thrown at the problems. But where are the vision, the courage, the leaders and the citizens determined to press for implementing a practical solution in our time?

It is my firm hope that we will witness a great sea change in attitudes to this problem over the next generation, for many of the broad themes in the discussion should now be plain. Freedom of thought, conscience, religion and belief is not a matter of freedom for the religious but a matter of human freedom. It is not about religion as a problem, but about how we live peacefully with our profound human differences. The starting point may sometimes be controversy and conflict, but the end goal is civility and the creation of a civil public square that maximizes freedom and justice for everyone. Such civility, and such a civil public square, must always be protected by law, but they must also be promoted, taught and transmitted as habits of the heart. There will never be a solution to the problem that is uniform and universal, but within the settlement each country chooses, there must be a steady expansion of the rights and freedoms protected for all and enjoyed by all—and so on and so on.

It is up to the next generation of global leaders and citizens to rise to the challenge. The United States, Europe and other countries in the West must take the lead in a determined expansion of soul freedom for all, and a careful building of civil public squares in each society. If they succeed, they can demonstrate the pattern and precedent for laying the foundations for a civil public square on the global level that may one day help shape the world. Present advances in information technology are opening up undreamed-of possibilities for human relations. But as recent events in China and Iran show clearly, this hi-tech potential can be turned toward repression as easily as toward freedom. If we wish to see the better outcome, we must make sure that new and constructive political thinking keeps pace with technological advances. The new capacities of the wired world must be channeled toward freedom, civility and persuasion rather than to prejudice, hatred and repression.

WHEN LEADERS LEAD

To many people the "religious problem" appears hopeless and intractable, made all the worse by the global resurgence of religion and the rise of religious extremism. But this is simply a way of saying that no one has been willing to address it with leadership and courage. The combined thrust of all we have discussed points in a more positive direction and represents a call to revaluation and action that must not be missed. But what would it take to affect a sea change in new national attitudes and eventually global attitudes? What could set national policies on a more constructive road and hold out the example of a new way for the world?

First, the world needs an assertion of courageous and visionary leadership, and in particular a partnership between far-sighted leaders from both the religious and the secularist sides. Could such leadership come from the American president, the German chancellor or the prime minister or foreign secretary of Britain, France, Canada, Australia or any of the other Western nations? Could it even come from a far-sighted leader in a Muslim-majority nation, as the late President Wahid of Indonesia promised to be before his untimely death?

It is unquestionable that wise people need a wise view of the place of religion in human affairs. For one thing, it is a simple fact that religion is the prime, as well as the most popular, source of human meaning and belonging throughout history and today. And it is hard to avoid the conclusion that just as culture drives politics, so religion drives culture. Religion, in short, is an enduring global reality, and one that for better or worse is unlikely to go away. It must therefore be faced squarely and understood wisely. New atheist hopes of "the end of faith" are as irrational as the beliefs of any "faith head" that they attack so truculently.

COBELLIGERENCE?

Would that across the world we had such leaders to match the hour, or even one or two to take the lead! But this vision and this proposal need not to wait for world leaders. In light of present realities another way forward is through a partnership between thoughtful secularists and thoughtful religious believers. The two sides may disagree profoundly over the religious and ideological differences between them, but they can still be cobelligerents on behalf of soul freedom, civility and a civil public square.

Precision is important here, and it is essential to be clear about the difference between an improper *secularist* state, which establishes or favors believers in a secularist worldview, and a proper *secular* state, which protects the foundational freedom of all believers, whether religious or secularist.

Such a partnership between religious and secularist believers might seem unlikely, but no other single combination of partners would have the same chance of breaking the stalemate in the culture wars and demonstrating an open horizon for new opportunities and solutions. And the time is ripe for just such an unlikely partnership. Consider the following seven points:

1. *Modern liberal secular societies depend on the solidarity of their*

citizens. The greater the liberty they enjoy and the wider the diversity they contain, the more important the question of the unity, or the social bond, which holds them together. It is a special challenge to sustain a stable and united society under the conditions of modern liberty and diversity. To be both positive and strong, this solidarity must be built on more than law and technology.

2. *Modern liberal secular societies depend on normative assumptions that they themselves cannot generate or guarantee.* Reason cannot justify itself by reason alone, and in the same way a truly neutral state cannot justify itself by purely neutral values. Both reason and the liberal state must therefore become aware of their own limitations and realize that they have to look to sources outside themselves for their foundations.

3. *Modern liberal secular societies have risen and still depend on philosophical and ethical traditions that come from outside themselves.* As a matter of simple, historical record, most of these indispensable foundations of freedom, justice and virtue are prepolitical and religious in character. The secular state therefore depends on more than the secular.

4. *Naturalistic or secularist worldviews are traditions limited to certain classes and social locations just as different religious worldviews are.* Like all others, such worldviews are simply one set of core beliefs and worldviews among many. They have the right to every right, but no right to be privileged above any others, and no more right to be universalized today than religious worldviews were in the past. The liberal secular state in particular has no right to attempt to privilege secularist beliefs.

5. *Modern liberal secular societies in the West should be viewed as postsecularist just as much as post-Christian.* The Christian consensus of the European and early American past has gone, but the myth of the purely and strictly secularist state has been shown up starkly too. The modern state is a multifaith state, in the sense that

religious diversity is a social fact. It is therefore in the interests of the liberal state to pay due attention to the full range of the voices of its citizens and of the sources of its norms and its solidarity. Religious believers of all kinds make important claims to truth as well as important contributions to society, so their rights should be respected and their voices heard if the state is truly to be open, free, liberal and democratic.

6. *History contains examples of the dark pathology of secularism as well as religion, and proponents of each should acknowledge these pathologies with candor and humility.* Both have brought blessings and both have brought curses to the story of civilization, and the balance sheet of each should be assessed accurately and fairly.

7. *The relationship of religious and secularist believers is critical to the future of modern liberal secular societies, especially as they relate in public life.* If their antagonism is not to prove the undoing of liberal democracy, they must come together as partners in the common cause of freedom, justice and humanity. Nothing is more urgent for democratic societies than the forging of a civil and cosmopolitan public square that does justice to the interests of both partners in the relationship.

If leaders and citizens can agree on these points, or at least accept them as talking points on an agreed agenda, then we may begin a fruitful conversation without suspicion and without rancor. Eventually, a fruitful partnership may emerge. Most people who have engaged issues that deal with religion in public life or with freedom of conscience have at times experienced venomous hostility from one extreme or the other. I myself, when leading the project of the Williamsburg Charter, a bicentennial celebration of the religious liberty clauses of the U.S. Constitution, received death threats for six months.

It is no secret, too, that the discussion of religion in educated circles today is often so sour that even a modest proposal such as this would be swept off the table with yet another karate chop of the culture warrior's rhetoric. Yet that is still my proposal: a partnership between thoughtful believers and secularists, working on behalf of humanity and freedom in the global era—with full respect for the integrity of each, but with an eye to wider human flourishing.

Only such courageous leadership can step in between the culture warriors, the fear-mongers, the alarmists and the fomenters of hatred and call for the fighting to cease. Only such a costly leadership would have a chance of calling each side to lay down its arms and be prepared to pay the price of taking the hatred into itself. Only such a creative leadership would be able to embody the vision of a robust and rights-respecting civility that knows how to disagree without being disagreeable or dismissive.

ATTUNED TO THE WIDER WORLD

Second, there needs to be a retooling of international diplomacy to make it capable of doing justice to the religious factor. Earlier, I argued that the West was making a mistake to view freedom of religion and belief as a matter for international relations only. The immediate challenge lies in expanding freedom of religion and belief for all within the West itself. But international diplomacy is vital too.

The intelligence community is the eyes and ears of the nation-state, providing it with the reliable information necessary for wise diplomacy and sound international relations. Any factor that obscures those perceptions is therefore a potentially disastrous handicap. It might be caused by the myopia brought on by narrow special interest groups, the biases born of political correctness and groupthink—or the handicap of being religiously tone deaf. But the effect is the same. Trying to cover today's world without understanding religion is as gauche as sending a tone deaf reporter to cover a Wagner opera.

The European Union's refusal to mention its own religious history in the preamble to its constitution is a glaring example of such a blind spot, but the problem runs far wider. It has been argued that despite their major differences, each of the three main American foreign policy schools—the realist, the liberal internationalist and the neoconservative—has a striking deficiency in their views of religion in global affairs. For the realists, religion is merely another expression of the drive to power. For the liberal internationalists, religion is a roadblock of tradition that stands in the way of liberal progress, as they define it. And for the neoconservatives, religion is an unwelcome intruder that trails a long way behind economic and military factors in the discussion of what really counts.

The result is a Pentagon-sized deficit in understanding that is a hole in the heart of American foreign policy, both culpable and disastrous. Madeleine Albright remarked that when she was secretary of state, she had hundreds of experts at her beck and call when it came to economic advice, but only one with expertise on religion— Ambassador Robert Seiple. She recommended that an expert on religion be attached to the desk of every country the State Department deals with in which the religious factor is significant for better or worse. But her recommendation has fallen on deaf ears, and the tendency has been for the ambassadors since then to be steadily sidelined and marginalized beyond usefulness.

At a higher level there should be a fresh consideration of the proposal for a Faith and Diplomacy Task Force that would act in an advisory capacity to the United Nations Security Council, and help to prevent and resolve religiously based conflicts. This could be a religious counterpart to the notion of global elders. Senator John Danforth first put forward the idea of such a task force when he was the U.S. ambassador to the United Nations under President George W. Bush. Not surprisingly the idea received a warm welcome in many parts of the world where the religious factor was taken seriously. But it was eventually shot down—and not by a secularist regime such as China, Cuba or North Korea, but by the U.S. State Department. Despite vigorous advocacy from the National Security Council of the time, the tone deaf won the day. They could not hear the music, and they did not see the point.

In short, wise foreign policy must know how to address and deploy religion intelligently. At the very least, wherever religion is part of a problem, religion must be part of the solution.

ESSENTIALS FOR THE TASK

Third, there are three requirements for anyone who would work toward such a vision of global civility, and no one part can be successful without the others, as can be seen from the lessons of the better angels of the American experiment.

First, there has to be the *moral suasion* of a declaration (as in the Magna Carta, the Declaration of Independence, the Bill of Rights, the Rights of Man and Citizen and the Universal Declaration of Human Rights).

Second, moral suasion has to be followed by the *legal implementation* of the rights expressed in laws (as in the U.S. Constitution and the many countries that have enacted the articles of the Universal Declaration of Human Rights into their constitutions or their laws).

Third, there has to be a process of ongoing *education and transmission* of the rights and responsibilities from one generation to the next (as in what used to be called liberal or civic education).

In the present litigious mood of many of the world's societies, the only one of the three that most people think of automatically is the second: legal implementation. But there is a crying need for the first and third parts too. The first part concerns a global declaration of the rights and responsibilities of freedom of conscience. This is what follows in *The Global Charter of Conscience*, published in Brussels at the Parliament of the European Union in 2012. It reaffirms Article 18 of the Universal Declaration of Human Rights and expands on it to affirm soul freedom for all and for the good of all, and to do justice to the conditions and challenges of living with our deepest differences today.

As for the third part, it was once understood that, while everyone in a free society is born free, no one is automatically worthy of and equal to freedom. There therefore needs to be education for liberty, or "liberal education," if a free society is to cultivate the habits of the heart that are essential to its endurance. Such civic education on behalf of soul freedom and civility is also conspicuously missing in the United States and in many parts of Europe and other Western countries.

Again, let there be no misunderstanding. I am emphatically not arguing for a one-size-fits-all settlement of religion and public life. Freedom of thought, conscience, religion and belief is a universal right that can be implemented from country to country in different local ways. Each country has the duty and the right to develop its own settlement according to its own history, its own values and its own heritage.

But I am arguing that, whatever the chosen settlement, each country should pursue two things. First, there should be a steady expansion of the protection and promotion of basic and inalienable rights within the settlement. And second, there should be a determination to expand the sphere of the civil public square to maximize freedom and justice for the good of all citizens. The overall principle is clear: The greater the eventual protection and practice of freedom of thought and conscience for all, the greater the promotion of civility and the greater the realization of justice and liberty.

Is such a vision of a civil and cosmopolitan global public square utopian and as forlorn as Kant's "perpetual peace"? Time will tell, though it is no more utopian than the American founders' audacity in breaking with fifteen hundred years of European established churches and setting out a new and "true remedy" in the teeth of centuries of experience of church-state and state-church oppression. After all, as Madison claimed to Harriet Martineau, the United States has always been useful in proving things before held impossible.[4]

Many people think that the United States would be the most likely candidate to take the lead in establishing a civil public square as a precedent for the world. With its rich history in this field, America should have the best chance of building such a civil public square today. Were that to happen, it would be the natural fruition of two and a third centuries of rich resources and practical lessons—including the negative lessons of the violations of freedom, ranging from the anti-Catholic riots in the early nineteenth century to the current culture warring.

There are strong reasons to conclude, however, that the United States will blindly continue its internecine culture wars and therefore miss such an opportunity, bent ferociously on betraying its heritage and forfeiting its natural leadership over this issue. Will Americans, leaders and citizens, forfeit this historic opportunity and allow that to happen? Only a little while ago that would have been unthinkable, such was the statesmanship that seemed natural and effortless to Americans after the Second World War. But that was then. Such is the surly, shortsighted and suicidal mood in America today that the unthinkable is all too possible.

Let the Americans rise to the moment or squander their heritage as they choose. That too is their right. What their failure means is that other nations, with less precedent but greater awareness of the contemporary urgency, could take the lead—the European Union, for example, where the issue is crucial to the future of its entire transnational experiment. With nearly fifty member states and 800 million people, the European Union now offers the largest and most successful framework for human rights protection in the world, and its need to know how to balance its diversity with its unity is obvious.

It is conceivable that a practical solution might emerge first, not in the America but in Western Europe and the other parts of the English-speaking world, such as Australia, Canada and New Zealand. Many of the first principles are already present there, at least in the English-speaking world that is the heir of what Edmund Burke called the "ancient liberties" of the English. To this point these liberties have not been thought through and have never flowered in these countries to the extent they have in the United States. But there is no reason why they should not.

Recent history shows, however, that most European discussion of human rights has been strong in its emphasis on law but lacking in any appreciation of the importance of Tocqueville's habits of the heart. Besides, some of the early attempts to find solutions, such as the British and Dutch responses to immigration through an ill-considered social philosophy of state multiculturalism, have proved disastrously counterproductive. They simply did not think through the character of freedom, and especially of freedom of thought and conscience, and some of their more recent policies have been little better. Their next attempts will have to show a better sense of history and a firmer grasp of the first principles of religious freedom.

In some long day ahead, perhaps, if the free, open societies of the West chart their course strongly, the same vision of soul freedom and a truly civil public square could spread even farther. It may even be considered by countries that are now rocked by violence, torn by religious conflicts or stifled by government repression, and with no present cultural resources to undergird true human rights—even in China and the Middle East. At the moment, however, if imitation is the best form of flattery, the West has little to be flattered for when it comes to resolving this issue. But Madison's "true remedy" is there to be restored, and the world conditions are crying out for such a restoration.

BEACON, BENCHMARK AND BLUEPRINT

Mention of the Universal Declaration of Human Rights provides a helpful reminder, a concluding challenge and sober warning. Sixty years after the passing of the declaration in Paris, December 1948, its historic stature is unquestionable. Standing in the shining tradition of the Magna Carta in 1215, the English Bill of Rights in 1688, the Virginia Declaration of Rights in May 1776, the Declaration of Independence in July of that year, the French Declaration of the Rights of Man and of the Citizen in 1789, and the U.S. Bill of Rights in 1791, the Universal Declaration of Human Rights is the greatest and most influential declaration of human rights and freedoms in history.

At the same time, the Universal Declaration has coexisted with such horrific slaughters as Mao's Cultural Revolution, Pol Pot's Killing Fields and the Rwanda massacre.

Do such atrocities make the Universal Declaration null and void, as critics have charged? Far from it. They serve to underscore its urgency. But more importantly, the entire world—the West as well as the rest, the powerful as much as those below them—has now been put on notice that no one is above the law, and that anyone can now find themselves defendants before the bar of the world if they flout and trample the rights of their fellow human beings.

To be sure, the Universal Declaration was a declaration of purely moral suasion, which only later was accorded legal implementation in certain countries and still awaits the education and transmission it deserves. But this does not undercut its significance.

As a ringing declaration of moral suasion, the Universal Declaration of Human Rights was a beacon, a benchmark and a blueprint. As a beacon, it expresses the highest human aspirations of human dignity, freedom and justice. As a benchmark, it enables the most rigorous practical assessments of how different nations are matching up to these rights. And as a blueprint, it empowers the most creative implementation of these rights in nations that wish to respect such rights and take their stand among the rights-respecting or duty-bearing citizens of the earth.

Yet this mention of the Universal Declaration also carries a sober warning. Like the Bretton Woods financial system agreed in New Hampshire in 1944, the Universal Declaration in Paris in 1948 owed much to its unique postwar setting. In the case of the Universal Declaration, a vital factor in its passing was the worldwide revulsion against the Nazi atrocities and the anger and impatience at the weakening but still powerful European empires.

Six decades on, such factors have disappeared, the unity of the West has collapsed, and the global strength and moral stature of the United States have slipped beyond recall. For all the courage and brilliance of its pioneers, such as Lebanon's Charles Malik and America's Eleanor Roosevelt, not to speak of its powerful influence since 1948, the Universal Declaration of Human Rights could never pass in today's circumstances. And the problem does not lie solely with the newly emerging power of Chinese communist totalitarianism and the oil-rich strength of reactionary Islam in the Middle East. It also stems from many of the intelligentsia in the West who are playing their part in undermining the basis, the universality and the inclusiveness of the Universal Declaration.

Is the Universal Declaration to be eroded, article by article, violation by violation and claimed alternative by claimed alternative? Will the Declaration one day be assigned to the dust heap of history, no more serious and no more lasting than the high-minded humanitarianism of Alexander the Great's famous oath at Opis in 324 B.C.? The importance of reaffirming and extending the message of the Universal Declaration today is urgent, even dire. In the relativistic climate of postmodernism and the reactionary mood of postcolonialism, with Chinese communists rejecting human rights point blank and Muslim nations and organizations pressing for rights that favor Islam above all, the very basis, the universality and the inclusiveness of the Universal Declaration are all equally under threat.

The accomplishments of a global project on behalf of freedom of thought, conscience, religion and belief for people of all faiths and no faiths are therefore all the more urgent. What is now required is global leadership in concert with visionary leaders and concerned citizens across the world. It is often said that a failure of leadership meant that Woodrow Wilson's vision of a "world safe for democracy" produced "the war to end all wars," and then "the peace to end all peace." John Kennedy's vision in June 1963 of a "world safe for diversity" has hung in the air unfulfilled for a different reason—five short months after the ringing declaration was issued, its bearer was cut down by an assassin's bullet.

Now, more than six decades after the Universal Declaration of Human Rights and more than five decades after President Kennedy's call, it is time, and past time, for the world to pick up the torch again. Wiser because of the mixed but finally glorious lessons of the slow, painful protection of freedom of thought and conscience, global leaders can demonstrate to the world how to do justice to liberty, diversity and harmony together, and thus help build a world of tomorrow that is truly safer for diversity, and therefore for human flourishing.

As I began this essay, we are now seven billion humans jostling together on our tiny planet earth, and we face a triple challenge that will be a key to our human future: Do we have reason enough to believe in the dignity and worth of every last one of us? Is there a way to live with the deepest religious and ideological differences that divide us? And are we able to settle our deliberations and debates through reasoned persuasion rather than force, intimidation and violence? Will we, in short, do justice to the dictates of our humanity?

The deepest answers to each of these questions lie in an exploration of soul freedom for all. Will the next generation learn from the best and worst of the past, will it rise to the challenge of the future and will it ensure the soul freedom for all that is essential to human flourishing? We are frequently told that where there is a will, there is a way. In this case there is a way, a way that is sure, clear, constructive and eminently feasible—the logical extension of the highest ideals and most sound political arrangements that brave men and women have pioneered before us. Our question today is a different one: Where there is a way, is there a will? The world awaits the answer to that question.

THE GLOBAL CHARTER
OF CONSCIENCE

THE FOLLOWING GLOBAL CHARTER OF CONSCIENCE was published in Brussels at the European Parliament in June 2012, with the endorsement of the United Nations rapporteur for religious freedom. It was drafted to reaffirm and support Article 18 of the Universal Declaration of Human Rights.

As such, it affirms the rights and responsibilities of freedom of thought and conscience for people of all faiths, all societies and all times. The open assumption of this declaration is that freedom of thought, conscience, religion and belief is universal, mutual and reciprocal, and therefore, without exception, for the good of all. Indeed, the full imperative for such freedom and such a right is that they are about nothing less than the freedom and responsibility to be fully human.

Everyone has the right to freedom of thought, conscience
and religion; this right includes freedom to change his religion or belief, and freedom, either in community with
others and in public or private, to manifest his religion or
belief in teaching, practice, worship, and observance.

—Universal Declaration of Human Rights, Article 18

The General Assembly proclaims this Universal Declaration
of Human Rights as a common standard of achievement for
all peoples and all nations, to the end that every individual
and every organ of society, keeping this Declaration constantly in mind, shall strive by teaching and education to
promote respect for these rights and freedoms and by progressive measures, national and international, to secure their
universal and effective recognition and observance, both
among the peoples of member states themselves and among
the peoples of territories under their jurisdiction.

—Universal Declaration of Human Rights,
Paris, December 1948

- The Global Charter of Conscience -

*A Global Covenant Concerning Faiths
and Freedom of Conscience*

Keenly aware of the titanic promise and peril of our time, as forms of global interconnectedness reach an unprecedented speed, scale, and scope across the earth, we issue and subscribe to this Charter to address a major world challenge whose resolution will be decisive for the cause of civilization and human flourishing. That is, we address the urgent problems raised by the challenge of "living with our deepest differences" when those differences involve core beliefs, worldviews, and ways of life, and when they are increasingly found within single communities, nations, and civilizations.

Our purpose is to set out a vision of the rights, responsibilities, and respect that will be the foundation of a civil and cosmopolitan "global public square," and the habits of the heart for those who would be "citizens of the world" as well as patriots in their own countries, and so to advance the cause of a "good world" and thus of global civilization over against the forces of global chaos.

Preamble

Whereas a fundamental feature of our human life is the characteristic drive for meaning and belonging;

Whereas for most people in most of history, and still today, this drive for meaning and belonging has been satisfied through ultimate beliefs and worldviews, whether supernatural or secular, transcendent or naturalistic;

Whereas religious and naturalistic beliefs and worldviews have inspired some of the best and some of the worst human attitudes and behavior throughout history—the worst including terrible examples of prejudice, hatred, conflict, persecution, censorship, repression, crimes against humanity and genocide that stain the pages of the human record;

Whereas the challenge of living with our deepest differences has been raised to a new level of intensity in the modern global era because of the flow of people and ideas, and especially the impact of the media, travel, and the migration of peoples, so that it is now said that "everyone is everywhere" and diverse beliefs and worldviews are both in constant contact and interdependent;

Whereas the world is witnessing two opposing trends—the revitalization and growing political influence of religious orthodoxies, with the danger of attempts to retain the supremacy of one religion at the expense of others, and the spread of naturalistic worldviews, with the equal danger of excluding all religions from public life and thus favoring secularism—and as a result, many of the traditional settlements of religion and public life show signs of stress and a need to be renegotiated;

Whereas the many trends of the advanced modern era—such as global communications, migrations, multicultural diversity, and the revolutions of science and technology—indicate that ethically contentious issues are likely to increase rather than diminish, and to demand clear values and wise solutions that transcend the conflicts between religions and secularism;

Whereas there is a grave awareness of the terrible specter of weapons of mass destruction in the hands of violent extremists;

Whereas there are leaders and peoples in the world who in either theory or practice still deny the universality and equality of human rights to all human beings;

Whereas the idea of "the public square," where citizens may come together to deliberate and decide issues of common public life, has long been precious and vital to peoples who value freedom and desire to take responsibility for their own lives and political affairs;

Whereas modern global communications, and above all, the Internet, have expanded the notion of public life and created the possibility of an emerging "global public square;"

Whereas ultimate beliefs of all sorts have a primary and positive role in the diverse movements and organizations representing burgeoning civil society around the world;

Whereas human dignity, justice, and order are the necessary foundations for free and peaceful societies;

Whereas the history of human affairs is the story of the conflict between Right and Might, and between Reason and Conscience on one side and of Power and Interest on the other;

Whereas the Universal Declaration of Human Rights has become the most influential statement of rights in human history, and therefore the champion of reason and conscience in the Age of Rights and in the long human struggle to realize freedom, justice, and peace on earth;

Declaration

We therefore set out the following declarations on faiths, civility, and peace on earth, to supplement and provide unreserved support for *The Universal Declaration of Human Rights* (The United Nations Assembly, Paris, December, 1948), and in particular to support Article 18 of *The Universal Declaration,* which reads: "Everyone has the right to freedom of thought, conscience and religion; this right includes freedom to change his religion or belief, and freedom, either alone or in community with others and in public or private, to manifest his religion or belief in teaching, practice, worship and observance."

Fundamental Freedom

Article 1. Freedom of conscience, or religious liberty, is a precious, fundamental, and inalienable human right—the right to adopt, hold, freely exercise, share, or change one's beliefs, subject solely to the dictates of conscience and independent of all outside, especially governmental control. This freedom includes all ultimate beliefs and worldviews, whether supernatural or secular, transcendent or naturalistic.

Birthright of Belonging

Article 2. This right to freedom of conscience, or religious liberty, is inherent in humanity and rooted in the inviolable dignity of each human individual, in particular in the character of reason and conscience. As a birthright of belonging, freedom of conscience is the equal right of all human beings regardless of their religion, gender, race, class, language, political or other opinion, or nationality, and regardless of any mental and physical handicap and any social, economic, or educational deprivation.

Freedom of conscience is the right of believers, not beliefs, and a protection for individuals rather than ideas.

Independent of Governments and Majorities

Article 3. As a right that is inherent in humanity and in the dignity of the human person, freedom of conscience does not finally depend on the discoveries of science, the favors of the state and its officials, or the changing will of majorities. It is therefore not a government's right to grant or to deny, but a government's responsibility to guarantee and guard. Human rights are a bulwark against all undue interference and control of the human person.

Integral and Essential

Article 4. Freedom of conscience is among the oldest of the human rights, and a primary and essential human right that is integral and essential to other basic rights and may not be sundered from them. Just as the right of freedom of assembly assumes and requires the right of freedom of expression, so the right of freedom of expression assumes and requires the right of freedom of conscience. Freedom of conscience, or religious liberty, is therefore far more than liberty for the religious: it is a core right for all human beings. While there are different systems for the protection of human rights, there are no alternative systems of human rights, but an equal and universal system of rights for all human beings and the whole world. Without respect for rights, human dignity withers. Without respect for human dignity, there can be no justice. And without respect for justice, there can be no true and lasting peace on earth.

Yardstick of Freedom

Article 5. Freedom of thought, conscience, and religion, or freedom of religion or belief, protects different aspects of religious freedom that are integral, interlocking and essential for a full understanding of freedom. To the extent that a society protects all these aspects of freedom for people of all faiths and none, it may be considered free and just, for freedom too is an aspect of social justice. Conversely, to the extent that a society refuses to protect any or all of these aspects of freedom, it forfeits its claim to freedom and justice.

Double Protection

Article 6. Freedom of conscience is among the civil and political rights enumerated in *The Universal Declaration of Human Rights,* but it must not be separated from the social and economic rights also enumerated. Both together serve the fundamental requirements for just and free societies. The former protects the dignity and freedom of the human individual, whereas the latter protects the solidarity and justice of human society.

Foundation of Society

Article 7. Freedom of conscience is fundamental for societies as well as for individuals, because it serves both as a protection for individual citizens and as a prerequisite for ordering the relationship of religions, ideologies and public life. This is especially important in today's world where pluralism makes religious liberty more necessary, just as religious liberty makes pluralism more likely.

Unconditional

Article 8. The right to freedom of conscience is absolute and unlimited in terms of belief, though not in terms of practice. No human being should therefore suffer discrimination, persecution, penalties, imprisonment, or death because of beliefs with which others disagree. In terms of practice, this right is limited because of the equal rights of others on whom practices impinge. The constant negotiation between the rights and responsibilities of each citizen and the wider common good is an ongoing challenge for societies that would be both just and free.

Rights and Responsibilities

Article 9. The right to freedom of conscience, or religious liberty, contains a duty as well as a right, an obligation and not only an entitlement, because a right for one person is automatically a right for another and a responsibility for both. All citizens are responsible for the rights of all other citizens, just as others are responsible for theirs. A society is only as just and free as it is respectful of this right, especially toward the beliefs of its smallest minorities and least popular communities.

Golden Rule

Article 10. The principle that the right to freedom of conscience is inalienable and equal for all represents the universal Golden Rule for religious liberty, and underscores the importance of the reciprocity of rights in different societies and nations. There are no rights exclusive to any privileged religion, worldview, or group. Any assertion of a claim to rights with respect to faith, whether in regard to freedom to believe, or to worship, or to build places of worship, or to convert others, automatically requires the claimants to offer that same right to people of all other faiths.

The Rights of Believers in Association

Article 11. The rights of freedom of conscience apply not only to individuals, but to individuals in community with others, associating on the basis of faith. Each person treasures the rights that inhere as in their person as an individual. Equally, each person treasures membership in families, communities, religious groups, and other deep affiliations. The rights of peoples in association are membership rights, and they are as meaningful and significant as the rights we enjoy as individuals.

No community of faith has rights that are superior to any other community, but the rights of thought, conscience, and religion are rights both for individuals and individuals in community because belief is both an individual assent and an associative practice. As such, religious groups must be free to govern their internal affairs free from governmental interference in questions of doctrine, selection of leaders, design of organizational polity, the admission and dismissal of members, and the future direction of the organization or community.

No One Settlement

Article 12. Each community, nation, or civilization is free to forge its own unique settlement of the relationship of religions, worldviews, and public life, and will do so naturally in light of its own history and its own culture. There is therefore no single, uniform settlement to be agreed upon by all, or imposed on all. But at the same time, diverse local settlements of religion and public life should embody the common universal rights and principles that are the hallmark of rights-respecting peoples everywhere. According to their success or failure to recognize and implement these rights in their local situation, communities, nations, and civilizations may be judged as more or less just, and more or less free.

Beware False Ordering

Article 13. An undeniable lesson of history is that the greatest threat to freedom of conscience is when the ordering of religion and government becomes coercive and oppressive to those who do not share the official views. This happens especially when government uses the mantle of an ultimate belief, or when an ultimate belief uses the power of government to coerce conscience and compel belief. This problem persists today when religious tests are used to proscribe speech or to bar individuals from political office; or when even moderate forms of religious or secularist settlement deny or curtail the rights of those within their society who hold different beliefs and worldviews; or when a state uses laws and actions to discriminate against religious minorities.

Dignity of Difference

Article 14. Freedom of conscience means that human diversity represents a dignity of difference as well as a danger in difference, though there is always a responsibility to find common ground across the differences without compromising the differences that matter. Rightly respected and ordered, diversity based on the dignity of difference is positive and can lead to richness, strength, and harmony in society, rather than to conflict, weakness, and disunity. In contrast, for a community or country to speak of harmony and diversity with no regard for religious liberty is a contradiction in terms and politically unsustainable in the age of global rights.

Differences Irreducible

Article 15. Freedom of conscience means there is a beneficial value but a definite limitation to the approach that seeks unity and resolution through dialogue and co-operation between religions and worldviews. In the end, the decisive differences between the world's ultimate beliefs are ultimate and irreducible—and these differences are crucial for both individuals and for societies and civilizations. This realistic recognition of the limits of dialogue is rooted in the constraints caused by deep commitments to truth claims.

Civil Public Square

Article 16. The public place of freedom of conscience in a world of deep diversity is best fulfilled through the vision of a cosmopolitan and civil public square—a public square in which people of all faiths, religious and naturalistic, are free to enter and engage public life on the basis of their faith, but always within a double framework: first, under the rule of law that respects all human rights, freedom of conscience in particular, and makes no distinction between peoples based on their beliefs; and second, according to a freely agreed covenant specifying what each person understands to be just and free for everyone else too, and therefore of the duties involved in living with the deep differences of others.

Conversation for the Common Good

Article 17. Among the responsibilities and duties required of citizens by virtue of their respect for freedom of conscience is engagement in public conversation over the common good, and a recognition that persuasion has replaced coercion in public debate. In particular, citizens who engage in public life require a willingness to listen to others, and an ability to persuade others in terms that are accessible and persuasive to them—recognizing always that it is persuasion that bridges the gap between personal beliefs and the public good, and that the more diverse a society is, the more persuasive individuals and groups must be if they wish their views to prevail in public life.

Articles of Peace

Article 18. This model of a civil public square attains its unity through articles of peace rather than articles of faith. Based on articles of peace, unity is forged through a framework of common rights, responsibilities, and respect, within which each faith and worldview is free to be faithful to its own beliefs and moral visions, yet also knows how to differ and live peacefully with the differences of others. Importantly, the model of a civil public square does not aim for a unity based on articles of faith. The dignity of difference and the fact of human diversity mean that unity can never be attained by a search for a lowest common denominator religious unity, or through interfaith dialogue.

Civil Society

Article 19. This declaration of the rights of freedom of conscience, and its accompanying vision of a civil public square, is vital to the flourishing of civil society. As individual societies and the whole world come to thrive through the energy and dedication of citizens engaging in a myriad of voluntary and nongovernmental organizations, it is necessary for them to have the freedom to express their moral visions in their chosen channels of voluntarism, philanthropy, reform, and social entrepreneurialism. A civil public square is therefore essential to a healthy civil society, just as a healthy civil society is vital for fostering a civil public square.

Peace Through Justice

Article 20. This declaration of the rights of freedom of conscience assumes that peace is more than the absence of conflict, and that peace through justice and the wise ordering of religion and public life is always better than peace through victory and the force of arms. Workable and lasting peace is not utopian, and does not envision the ending of all tyranny and the arrival of "perpetual peace" on earth. The human goods of justice and freedom are always hard won and maintained at a cost, but peace ordered through justice is the only peace that is a true foundation for human wellbeing.

Challenge to the Religious

Article 21. The rights of freedom of conscience, the realities of modern religious diversity, and the responsibilities of a civil public square all pose a particular challenge to the traditional standing of established, or monopoly religions. We live at a time when fewer and fewer countries are dominated by one religion or worldview, and all the beliefs of the world are either present or available everywhere. Among the major challenges to traditional religious believers are an acknowledgment of the past excesses and evils of religions, a recognition of the rights of other religious believers, and an equal regard for the rights of the increasing number of citizens who are secularist in their ultimate beliefs.

Challenge to the Secularists

Article 22. The same rights of freedom of conscience, the same realities of contemporary diversity, and the same responsibilities of a civil public square all pose an equally fundamental challenge to secularists and to the notion of strictly secular public life in which religion is excluded from public discussion and engagement. Among the major challenges to secularists are an acknowledgment of the role of secularism in many of the world's recent oppressions and massacres, an appreciation that the process of secularization is not necessarily inevitable or progressive, and a proper recognition of the rights of religious citizens in public life—the denial of which is illiberal, unjust, and a severe impoverishment of civil society.

First Step Only

Article 23. This declaration of the rights of freedom of conscience is foundational and necessary, but only the first step in furthering freedom of conscience in just and free societies. As a form of moral suasion, it must always be followed by a second step—legal implementation of the same rights in national and international law—and then by a third step: cultivating, through civic education and transmission, the habits of the heart that alone ensure that respect for rights and responsibilities are handed on from generation to generation. All three steps are needed for a society, or for the world, to achieve a genuine and lasting measure of justice and freedom.

Ongoing Questions

Article 24. As the history of *The Universal Declaration of Human Rights* shows, its powerful influence in advancing the Age of Rights has gone hand in hand with enduring questions and criticisms. In particular, there have been persistent challenges to the basis of its affirmations, to the universality of its claims, and to the inclusiveness of its reach—and thus to "the right to its rights." Because of the changing fortunes of human philosophies and the recurring fact of the deliberate abuse of human rights by certain authorities, such challenges will always persist and will always require a robust response, and by advocates of this Charter too, especially to the challenge to universality.

Claim to Universality

Article 25. The *Global Charter of Conscience* asserts its claim to universality in terms of its scope, though not its observance. It is universal in that it is grounded in the dignity and equality of all human beings, and it is addressed to all the citizens of the world, on behalf of all the rights-respecting citizens of today's world. We make this declaration with the full realization that to claim to speak from *nowhere* is impossible, and that to speak from *everywhere* is incoherent. We speak from *somewhere,* and in our own time, but with the sure confidence that these declarations, agreed on by people of many traditions and perspectives, are universal affirmations that speak to and for all human beings across all continents and all centuries—even to those who now resist the equality and universality of human rights.

Enduring Obstacles

Article 26. All declarations of human rights encounter enduring obstacles, above all the realities of human nature and the crooked timber of our humanity. Just as *The Universal Declaration of Human Rights* has advanced the cause of justice in the face of deliberate, flagrant, systematic, and continuing violations of human rights, so this Charter openly acknowledges that it will encounter similar challenges and opposition. Problems such as neglect, forgetfulness, hypocrisy, deliberate violations, and criminal abuses of human dignity and rights are both to be expected and resisted. Far from nullifying the rights asserted here, such violations highlight their character and importance.

First Principles Best

Article 27. This Charter of the rights of freedom of conscience starts and proceeds by the consideration of fundamental first principles. It therefore stands in strong contrast to other approaches to resolving problems of religious conflict that will always prove inadequate or dangerous because they ignore or bypass the primary rights of freedom of conscience, and the fact that freedom of conscience is a protection for believers, doubters, and skeptics, but not for beliefs.

Two such faulty approaches are especially common. On the one hand, some people view tolerance as the attitude of those who believe nothing and as the fruit of indifference toward faiths. On the other hand, some people believe that disagreement with, and criticism of other beliefs is innately intolerant. In response: Discourse concerning the ultimate beliefs of others must be respectful, but many critiques and caricatures are not "blasphemy" or "defamation." There must be a commitment to the equality of freedom of conscience for all. Like all human rights, freedom of conscience is the right of every human being without exception. There can be no human rights for some but not others.

All approaches that ignore the consequential character of ultimate beliefs in life and the primary place of freedom of conscience, and its rights, responsibilities, and respect, are inadequate for the proper defense of justice and freedom. Worse, such faulty approaches can also be dangerous, because either their motive or their unintended effect is to favor one religion or worldview at the expense of others, and so to undermine the equality and universality of the right of freedom of conscience in another way. It is never an advance in human rights when special protection for some people becomes oppression or discrimination for others. Nor when law is used to provide protection for a particular belief to the detriment of individuals who do not subscribe to that belief.

Pacesetter for Tomorrow

Article 28. The rights of freedom of conscience and the vision of a cosmopolitan and civil global public square are a crucial pacesetter and precedent for preventing global chaos and moving toward the governance of the global civilization of tomorrow. As globalization has advanced and human interconnectedness has increased, it is evident that global communications and global economics have far outstripped global politics. What global governance will mean in the future is not yet clear. But if the world is to respect both diversity and universality, and justice is to balance freedom in the search for peace, then a cosmopolitan and civil public square is a necessary stepping stone toward the global governance that is to come.

No Final Word

Article 29. The stern verdict of time on all human endeavour is "This too shall pass," which means that the wisest and best intentioned settlements of religion and public life are no more than the best so far. We therefore acknowledge humbly that this Charter is neither perfect, nor final, nor agreed by all. It represents our best current judgment as to the place of the rights of freedom of conscience in our world. But it is always open to future generations to improve and advance these affirmations, aiming always to build societies that are yet freer and more just, and thus more favorable to the highest human flourishing and the creation of a good world.

Conclusion

In conclusion, we issue *The Global Charter of Conscience* in the strong hope that, like *The Universal Declaration of Human Rights*, it will advance the cause of freedom of conscience and religious liberty for people of all faiths, religious or naturalistic. Our express goals for the Declaration are three:

First, that it will be a beacon expressing the highest human aspirations for freedom of thought, conscience, and religion.

Second, that it will be a benchmark enabling the most rigorous assessments of freedom of thought, conscience, and religion, which communities, countries, and civilizations have achieved so far.

Third, that it will be a blueprint empowering the most practical implementation of freedom of thought, conscience, and religion, in both law and civic education.

In sum, *The Global Charter of Conscience* is a response to a crucial and unavoidable part of the promise and peril of our time. Only by the wise and courageous application of these affirmations can humanity turn the danger of the differences between ultimate beliefs into a dignity of difference that will help "make the world safe for diversity."

ACKNOWLEDGMENTS

AFTER MANY DECADES OF WRESTLING with the challenges of freedom of thought, conscience, religion and belief, it would be impossible to mention all the people to whom I owe a special debt of gratitude. But it would be invidious not to mention the following:

Henry and Mary Guinness, my parents, who were my first models of courage in helping the poor and in standing without fear against murderous authorities in China during the war with Japan and the first years of the Chinese communist terror.

My Guinness ancestors and family heritage, to whom I owe my early stories of the ideal of nondiscrimination and of the importance of taking a stand for justice even against the practices of one's own country and civilization.

Peter Berger, David Martin, John Courtney Murray and Richard John Neuhaus, the former above all, who in different ways introduced me to the profound significance of religion in the global era and of a constructive way forward in a world of religiously based conflict and tension.

Bruce MacLaury, distinguished president of the Brookings Institution, who gave me the opening there that allowed me to do the thinking from which so much of my later work has grown.

The late Senator Ted Stevens and Catherine Stevens, whose

friendship and introductions launched a new arrival to the United States into a life of engaging with the thorny issues of religion and American public life.

John Seel, Bob Kramer, Al McDonald, Don Bonker, Tom McWhertor, Amy Boucher Pye, Peter Edman and Charles Haynes, whose collegiality and herculean labors, against many and sometimes surprising odds, made possible the accomplishments of the Williamsburg Charter. And to Steve Kennedy, whose friendship and scholarly sharpening have been an enduring source of stimulation and encouragement over many years.

John Mroz and Bud Smith, whose firm leadership and generous support at the EastWest Institute in New York led to the drafting of the Global Charter of Conscience.

Julia Doxat Purser, Christel Ngnambi, David Landrum, Thomas Schirrmacher, Geoffrey Tunnicliffe, Martyn Eden, Ian Smith and Gordon Showell Rogers, with whom it has been a privilege to work for a better way for religion and public life in the United Kingdom and Europe.

Bennett Graham and Benjamin Kafferlin, who have generously given me the benefit of their experience and their expertise in reading a draft of the manuscript, and in helping me to avoid mistakes and sharpen the completed book. Needless to say, the final result is mine, but it reads all the better for their excellent criticisms and helpful suggestions.

Nick and Sheila Nesland, for their generous hospitality in their magnificent home in Gig Harbor, Washington, that allowed me to complete the writing of this book.

Erik Wolgemuth, my friendly and tireless agent, who believed in me and in the ideas in this book when many others did not.

Al Hsu, Jeff Crosby, Alisse Wissman and all the wonderful team at InterVarsity Press, with whom it is a pleasure as well as stimulating to work together on a book.

Jenny and CJ, my family, whose constant love and support in pursuing what many thought utterly quixotic has been unfailing and decisive.

Notes

Chapter 1: The Golden Key

[1]See for example Brian J. Grim and Roger Finke, *The Price of Freedom Denied: Religious Persecution and Conflict in the 21st Century* (Cambridge: Cambridge University Press, 2012).

[2]See "Global Restrictions on Religion," Pew Forum on Religion and Public Life, December 2009, www.pewforum.org/uploadedFiles/Topics/Issues/Government/restrictions-fullreport.pdf.

[3]"Rising Tide of Restrictions on Religion," Pew Forum on Religion and Public Life, September 2012, www.pewforum.org/Government/Rising-Tide-of-Restrictions-on-Religion.aspx.

[4]Winston Churchill, *A History of the English-Speaking Peoples,* vol. 2, *The New World* (New York: Dodd, Mead, 1956).

[5]See for example Paul Marshall and Nina Shea, *Silenced: How Apostasy and Blasphemy Codes Are Choking Freedom Worldwide* (New York: Oxford University Press, 2012).

[6]See Timothy Samuel Shah, *Religious Freedom: Why Now?—Defending an Embattled Human Right* (Princeton, NJ: Witherspoon Institute, 2012).

[7]Philip Blom, *A Wicked Company* (New York: Basic Books, 2011), p. 293.

[8]John M. Barry, *Roger Williams and the Creation of the American Soul* (New York: Viking Penguin, 2012).

[9]Nina Shea, "The World's Worst Religious Persecutors," *National Review Online*, March 20, 2012, www.nationalreview.com/content/293960/world's-worst-religious-persecutors.

Chapter 2: For All the World

[1]Jonathan Sacks, *The Dignity of Difference* (New York: Continuum, 2002).

[2]Iain McGilchrist, *The Master and His Emissary* (New Haven, CT: Yale University Press, 2009), p. 460.

[3]Jonathan Sacks, *The Great Partnership: God, Science and the Search for Meaning* (London: Hodder & Stoughton, 2011), p. 12.

[4]Sam Harris, *The End of Faith: Religion, Terror, and the Future of Reason* (New York: W. W. Norton, 2004).

[5]John Adams, letter to Thomas Jefferson, April 19, 1817, in Lester J. Cappon, ed., *The Adams-Jefferson Letters: The Complete Correspondence Between Thomas Jefferson and Abigail and John Adams* (Chapel Hill: The University of North Carolina Press, 1959).

[6]"Rising Restrictions on Religion," Pew Forum on Religion and Public Life, August 9, 2011, www.pewforum.org/Government/Rising-Restrictions-on-Religion.aspx.

[7]Christopher Hitchens, *God Is Not Great: How Religion Poisons Everything* (New York: Grand Central Publishing, 2007).

[8]Blaise Pascal, *Pensées*.

[9]John Adams, letter to Thomas Jefferson, April 19, 1817. Quoted in Madeleine Albright, *The Mighty and the Almighty* (New York: HarperCollins, 2009), p. 65.

[10]Sacks, *Great Partnership*.

Chapter 3: A War of Spirits

[1]John Milton, *Areopagitica*, 1644.

[2]John Locke, *A Letter Concerning Toleration*, 1689.

[3]Friedrich Nietzsche, *Ecce Homo*, trans. R. J. Hollingdale (London: Penguin Classics, 1992), p. 97.

[4]Terry Eagleton, *Reason, Faith, & Revolution: Reflections on the God Debate* (New Haven, CT: Yale University Press, 2009), p. 140.

[5]Peter L. Berger, ed., *The Desecularization of the World: Resurgent Religion and World Politics* (Grand Rapids: Eerdmans, 1999), p. 2.

[6]Jose Casanova, "Globalization and the Free Exercise of Religion Worldwide," in *Challenges to Religious Liberty in the Twenty-First Century*, ed. Gerard V. Bradley (Cambridge: Cambridge University Press, 2012), p. 140.

[7]Ibid., p. 141.

[8]Ibid., p. 140.

[9]Christopher Dawson, *Progress and Religion: An Historical Inquiry* (Washington, DC: Catholic University of America Press, 2001), p. 177.

[10]Michael Nazir-Ali, *Triple Jeopardy for the West: Aggressive Secularism, Radical Islamism and Multiculturalism* (London: Bloomsbury, 2012).

[11]Bruno Waterfield, "Christians Should Leave Their Beliefs at Home or Get Another Job," *Daily Telegraph*, September 4, 2012, www.telegraph.co.uk/news/religion/9520026/Christians-should-leave-their-beliefs-at-home-or-get-another-job.html.

[12]Ibid.

Chapter 4: First Freedom First

[1]Thomas Jefferson, "Notes on the State of Virginia," in *Writings* (New York: Library of America, 1984), query 18, p. 237.

[2]John F. Kennedy, Inaugural Address, January 20, 1961.

[3]Richard Rorty, *Truth and Logic: Philosophical Papers* (Cambridge: Cambridge University Press, 1998), p. 172. Quoted in Andrew Clapham, *Human Rights: A Very Short Introduction* (Oxford: Oxford University Press, 2007), p. 14.

[4]Milan Kundera, *Immortality*, trans. Peter Kussi (New York: HarperCollins, 1999), p. 137. Quoted in Clapham, *Human Rights*, p. 17.

[5]Christopher Tollefsen, "Conscience, Religion, and the State," in *Challenges to Religious Liberty in the Twenty-First Century*, ed. Gerard V. Bradley (Cambridge: Cambridge University Press, 2012), pp. 113-14.

[6]Ibid., p. 114.

[7]John M. Barry, *Roger Williams and the Creation of the American Soul* (New York: Viking Penguin, 2012).

[8]Jean Jacques Rousseau, *The Social Contract* bk. 1, sec. 9, 1762.

[9]John Emerich Edward Dalberg-Acton, *The History of Freedom* (Fairford, UK: Echo Library, 2010), p. 41.

[10]Timothy Samuel Shah, *Religious Freedom: Why Now?—Defending an Embattled Human Right* (Princeton, NJ: Witherspoon Institute, 2012), p. 28.

[11]Michael W. McConnell, "The Problem of Singling Out Religion," *DePauw Law Review* 50 (2000): 42.

[12]Acton, *The History of Freedom*, p. 45.

[13]The Williamsburg Charter: A Reaffirmation of the First Amendment, 1988. See James Hutson, *The Founders on Religion* (Princeton, NJ: Princeton University Press, 2005), p. 165.

[14]Tertullian, *Apology* 24.6-10.

[15]Roger Williams, *The Bloudy Tenent of Persecution for the Cause of Conscience*, ed. Richard Greeves (Macon, GA: Mercer University Press, 2001), p. 3 (emphasis added).

[16]*The Collected Works of Walter Bagehot*, ed. Norman St. John-Stevas, vol. 6 (London: Oxford University Press, 1968–1986), p. 99; Jeremy Bentham, *Anarchical Fallacies* (1843). Quoted in Clapham, *Human Rights*, p. 11.

[17]Daniel Webster, speech at a public dinner in Concord, NH, September 30, 1834. Quoted in Frank Prochaska, *Eminent Victorians on American Democracy* (Oxford: Oxford University Press, 2012), p. 1.

[18]Barack Obama, speech at the Naval Academy Commencement, U.S. Naval Academy, Annapolis, MD, May 22, 2009. Quoted in Sheryl Gay Stolberg, "Obama Is Embraced at Annapolis," *New York Times,* May 23, 2009, A11.

[19]Hillary Clinton, speech on religious freedom, Carnegie Endowment for Peace, July 31, 2012.

[20]Welcome video, People of Faith for Obama, www.barackobama.com/people-of-faith.

[21]"Unacceptable," February 27, 2012, www.becketfund.org/wp-content/uploads/2012/02/Unacceptable-2-27-11am2.pdf.

[22]John Bingham and Tim Ross, "Christians 'Aren't Above the Law,' Says Equalities Chief Trevor Phillips," *Telegraph*, February 17, 2012, www.telegraph.co.uk/news/religion/9087775/Christians-arent-above-the-law-says-equalities-chief-Trevor-Phillips.html.

[23]See Roger Trigg, *Equality, Freedom and Religion* (Oxford: Oxford University Press, 2012), pp. 116-18.

[24]David P. Goldman, "Memo to Jews: After They Come for the Catholic Church, They Will Come for Us," *Spengler*, February 19, 2012.

[25]Michelle Obama, speech at the African Methodist Episcopal Church Conference, Nashville, June 28, 2012. Quoted in Ross Douthat, "Defining Religious Liberty Down," *New York Times,* July 28, 2012, www.nytimes.com/2012/07/29/opinion/sunday/douthat-defining-religious-liberty-down.html (emphasis added).

[26]See Leo Pfeffer, *Church, State and Freedom* (Boston: Beacon Press, 1953).

[27]Ghazi Ben Muhammad Ben Talal, welcome address to Pope Benedict XVI, Amman, Jordan, May 10, 2009.

[28]Paul Hawken, *Blessed Unrest* (New York: Penguin, 2007).

[29]Oliver Wendell Holmes, Dissenting Opinion, *Abrams v. United States* (1919). Quoted in Rodney A. Smolla, *Free Speech in an Open Society* (New York: Vintage Books, 1992), p. 6.

Chapter 5: Death by a Thousand Cuts

[1]Roger Williams, "The Bloudy Tenent of Persecution for the Cause of Conscience," in *The Complete Writings of Roger Williams* (New York: Russell and Russell, 1963), 3:306. Quoted in John M. Barry, *Roger Williams and the Creation of the American Soul* (New York: Viking Penguin, 2012), p. 58.

[2]*West Virginia State Board of Education v. Barnette* (1943).

[3]Jack Grimstone, "No Faith, Hope or Charity: Church Status in Jeopardy," *Sunday Times*, November 4, 2012, www.thesundaytimes.co.uk/sto/news/uk_news/Society/article1159173.ece.

[4]Roger Williams, *The Bloudy Tenent of Persecution for the Cause of Conscience*, ed. Richard Greeves (Macon, GA: Mercer University Press, 2001), chap. 74.

[5]James Madison, "Memorial and Remonstrance Against Religious Assessments," June 20, 1785, in *Selected Writings of James Madison*, ed. Ralph Louis Ketcham (Indianapolis: Hackett Publishing, 2006), p. 22.

[6]*Human Rights Review 2012*, Equality and Human Rights Commission, pp. 322, 323.

[7]Thomas Jefferson, "Notes on the State of Virginia," in *Writings* (New York: Library of America, 1984), p. 289.

[8]John Stuart Mill, *Essays on Politics and Society* (Toronto: University of Toronto Press, 1977), p. 66. Quoted in George Bancroft, *History of the Formation of the Constitution of the United States* (New York: Appleton, 1882), 1:3.

[9]Alexis de Tocqueville, *Democracy in America*, trans. Henry Reeve, ed. Francis Bowen (Cambridge, MA: Sever and Francis, 1863), 2:387. Quoted in Frank Prochaska, *Eminent Victorians on American Democracy* (Oxford: Oxford University Press, 2012), p. 31.

[10]Rodney A. Smolla, *Free Speech in an Open Society* (New York: Vintage Books, 1992), p. 10.

[11]Ibid., p. 11.

Chapter 6: Dueling Visions

[1]Omar Ahmad, quoted in Art Moore, "Did CAIR Founder Say Islam to Rule America? Muslims Confront Ohmar Ahmad as Newspaper Stands by Story," *WorldNetDaily.com*, December 11, 2006, www.wnd.com/2006/12/39229. (This Omar Ahmad quote is disputed—by Ahmad himself. He is supposed to have said it at a conference in 1998, but by the time the article cited here ran in 2006 there was no easy way to verify. This article cited here seems to be closest we can get to original source.)

[2]Johari Abdul-Malik, quoted in Andrew McCarthy, "More Moderate Muslims: For a Preview of the Ground Zero Mosque, Check Out Virginia," *National Review Online*, August 7, 2010, www.nationalreview.com/articles/243635/more-moderate-muslims-andrew-c-mccarthy.

[3]Ludwig Wittgenstein, quoted in Maurice O'Conner Drury, "Some Notes on Conversations with Wittgenstein," in *Recollections of Wittgenstein*, ed. Rush Rhees (Oxford: Oxford University Press, 1984), p. 102.

[4]Gottfried Leibnitz, quoted in Emil Brunner, *Christianity and Civilization*, Foundations, first part (London: Nisbet, 1947), p. 163.

[5]Eagleton, *Reason, Faith, & Revolution*, p. 110.

[6]Christopher Francis Patten, quoted in Jonathan Wynne-Jones, "Lord Patten Attacks 'Intolerant' Secularists," *Daily Telegraph*, April 24, 2011.

[7]See for example Stephen Greenblatt, *The Swerve: How the World Became Modern* (New York: W. W. Norton, 2011).

Chapter 7: Looking in the Wrong Place

[1]Thomas Farr, *World of Faith and Freedom: Why International Religious Liberty Is Vital to American National Security* (Oxford: Oxford University Press, 2008), p. 31.

[2]A. M. Rosenthal, "A Journalist's Year of Reawakening," *Sarasota Herald-Tribune*, December 31, 1997. Quoted in Paul Marshall, "Why Religious Freedom Must Be a Top Priority," *Cardus*, December 7, 2011.

[3]Ziya Meral, "The Giant Blind Spot of Human Rights NGOs," *Huffington Post*, October 2, 2011.

[4]William Shakespeare, *Hamlet*, act 1, scene 5.

[5]Max Planck, *Where Is Science Going?* trans. J. Murphy (London: Allen & Unwin, 1933), pp. 214, 217.

[6]Heraclitus, fragment 7, as quoted in *The Art and Thought of Heraclitus: A New Arrangement and Translation of the Fragments with Literary and Philosophical Commentary*, ed. Charles H. Kahn (Cambridge: Cambridge University Press, 1981), p. 31.

[7]Anthony Gill, *The Political Origins of Religious Liberty* (Cambridge: Cambridge University Press, 2008), p. 61.

[8]Andrew Clapham, *Human Rights: A Very Short Introduction* (Oxford: Oxford University Press, 2007), p. 29.

[9]Marie-Jean-Antoine-Nicolas Caritat, Marquis de Condorcet, The First Essay on the Political Rights of Women. A Translation of Condorcet's Essay "Sur l'admission des femmes aux droits de Cité" (On the Admission of Women to the Rights of Citizenship), trans. Dr. Alice Drysdale Vickery (Letchworth: Garden City Press, 1912).

[10]Confucius, *Analects* xv, section 23.

[11]Thomas Jefferson, *Notes on the State of Virginia* (Chapel Hill: University of North Carolina Press, 1955), p. 142.

[12]John M. Barry, *Roger Williams and the Creation of the American Soul* (New York: Viking Penguin, 2012), p. 393.

[13]Os Guinness, *A Free People's Suicide: Sustainable Freedom and the Future of America* (Downers Grove, IL: InterVarsity Press, 2012), p. 34.

[14]Samuel Johnson, quoted in Oliver Goldsmith, "The Traveller," in *The Poems and Plays of Oliver Goldsmith* (London: n.p., 1841), p. 4.

[15]Mary Ann Glendon, *Rights Talk: The Impoverishing of Political Discourse* (New York: Free Press, 1991), p. 2.

[16]George F. Will, "Obama's Disdain for Law," *Washington Post*, March 11, 2012, A19.

[17]Jean Jacques Rousseau, *The Social Contract*, bk. 1, sec. 7, 1762 (emphasis added).

[18]Henry de Bracton, *On the Laws and Customs of England*, ed. Samuel Edmund Thorne, vol. 2 (Cambridge, MA: Belknap Press of Harvard University Press, 1976), p. 27. Quoted in Barry, *Roger Williams and the Creation of the American Soul*, p. 31.

[19]George Weigel, "The Libertine Police State," *National Review Online*, February 13, 2012, www.nationalreview.com/content/290842/libertine-police-state.

[20]Adam Nossiter, "In Nigeria, a Deadly Group's Rage Has Local Roots," *New York Times*, February 25, 2012.

[21]Paul Berman, "Thought Police," *New Republic*, March 14, 2012.

[22]Timothy Garton Ash, "One Rule for Jesus, Another for Muhammad?" *Guardian*, March 14, 2012, www.guardian.co.uk/commentisfree/2012/mar/14/one-rule-jesus-another-muhammad.

[23]Ibid.

[24]Paul Marshall and Nina Shea, *Silenced: How Apostasy and Blasphemy Codes Are Choking Freedom Worldwide* (New York: Oxford University Press, 2012), p. 329.

[25]"Pakistan 'Koran Plot' Imam Remanded in Blasphemy Case," *BBC News Asia*, September 2, 2012, www.bbc.co.uk/news/world-asia-19454739.

[26]Pakistan Penal Code, section 295-C, 1986.

[27]Farahnaz Ispahani and Nina Shea, "Thwarting Religious Cleansing in the Muslim World," *National Review Online*, October 16, 2012, www.nationalreview.com/corner/330624/thwarting-religious-cleansing-muslim-world-farahnaz-ispahani.

[28]Declan Walsh, "Pakistani Minister Offers Bounty Over Anti-Islam Video," *New York Times*, September 22, 2012, www.nytimes.com/2012/09/23/world/asia/pakistani-minister-offers-bounty-over-anti-islam-video.html.

[29]"Salman Rushdie: Satanic Verses 'Would Not Be Published Today,' " BBC News, September 17, 2102, www.bbc.co.uk/news/entertainment-arts-19600879.

[30]Marshall and Shea, *Silenced*, p. 331.

[31]Rodney Smolla, *Free Speech in an Open Society* (New York: Vintage Books, 1992), p. 169.

[32]Julian Savulescu, "Conscientious Objection in Medicine," *British Medical Journal* 332 (February 2006): 294. Quoted in Christopher Tollefsen, "Conscience, Religion, and the State," in *Challenges to Religious Liberty in the Twenty-First Century*, ed. Gerard V. Bradley (Cambridge: Cambridge University Press, 2012), p.128.

[33]Glendon, *Rights Talk*, p. 9.

[34]See Christopher Lasch, *The Revolt of the Elites and the Betrayal of Democracy* (New York: W. W. Norton, 1996).

[35]Gracchus Babeuf, "Babeuf's Defense from the Trial at Vendôme, February–May 1797," in *Socialist Thought: A Documentary History*, ed. Albert Fried and Ronald Sanders (Chicago: Aldine, 1964), p. 67.

[36]A. C. Grayling, *Towards the Light* (London: Bloomsbury, 2007), p. 261.

[37]Roger Trigg, *Equality, Freedom, and Religion* (Oxford: Oxford University Press, 2012), p. 40.

[38]Alexis de Tocqueville, conversation with Nassau William Senior, May 22, 1850. In Alexis de Tocqueville with Nassau William Senior, *Correspondence & Conversations of Alexis de Tocqueville with Nassau William Senior from 1834 to 1859*, vol. 1, ed. M. C. M. Simpson (London: Henry S. King, 1872), p. 94.

[39]Benajmin Constant, *De l'espirit de conquête et de l'usurpation dans leurs rapports avec la civilization européenne*, together with *adolphe* (Paris: Gardier Freres, 1924 [?]), pp. xiii, 212.

[40]Thomas Babington Macaulay, letter to Henry S. Randall, May 23, 1857, printed in *The Southern Literary Messenger*, March 24, 1860.

[41]See Os Guinness, *The Case for Civility—And Why Our Future Depends on It* (San Francisco: HarperOne, 2008); David E. Campbell and Robert D. Putnam, "God and Caesar in America," *Foreign Affairs*, March–April 2012, pp. 34-43.

Chapter 8: A Civil and Cosmopolitan Public Square

[1]John Courtney Murray, SJ, *We Hold These Truths: Catholic Reflections on the American Proposition* (London: Sheed & Ward, 1960), p. 49.

[2]Roger Williams, *The Bloudy Tenent of Persecution for the Cause of Conscience*, ed. Richard Greeves (Macon, GA: Mercer University Press, 2001), p. 3. (See full quotation on p. 78 of this book.)

Chapter 9: Later Than We Think

[1]Sam Harris, *Free Will* (New York: Simon & Schuster, 2012). Quoted in Daniel Menaker, "Have It Your Own Way," *New York Times*, July 15, 2012, p. BR 20.

[2]Peter Singer, *Rethinking Life and Death: The Collapse of Our Traditional Ethics* (New York: Macmillan, 1996), p. 209.

[3]Peter Singer, *Writings on an Ethical Life* (New York: HarperCollins, 2001), pp. 160-61.

[4]James Madison, quoted in Harriet Martineau, *Society in America*, vol. 1 (Paris: A and W Galignani, 1837), p. 2. Quoted in Frank Prochaska, *Eminent Victorians on American Democracy* (Oxford: Oxford University Press, 2012), p. 20.

Name Index

SUBJECT INDEX